A Grammar of Freethought

by

Chapman Cohen

A Grammar of Freethought
by Chapman Cohen

ISBN: 978-93-61422-94-2

Published by

DOUBLE 9 BOOKS

2/13-B, Ansari Road
Daryaganj, New Delhi – 110002
info@double9books.com
www.double9books.com
Tel. 011-40042856

ABOUT THE AUTHOR

Chapman Cohen was an English freethinker, atheist, and secularist author and lecturer. Chapman Cohen was the older son of Enoch Cohen, a confectioner, and his wife, Deborah. He was born in Leicester, but the family relocated to London in 1889. He attended a nearby elementary school but was largely self-taught. He had read Spinoza, Locke, Hume, Berkeley, and Plato by the age of eighteen. He was a bibliophile who collected books throughout his life. Cohen described having "little religion at home and none at school" after being withdrawn from Religious Instruction lessons. He described his own attitude toward religion as "easy-going contempt". A few weeks later, he came out against the same lecturer on their invitation. Shortly after, he was invited to speak by the local National Secular Society chapter. After a year of speaking on freethought, he joined the NSS. In 1895, he was elected as vice-president of the NSS. Cohen began submitting weekly essays to G. W. Foote's Freethinker in 1897, after previously writing on his lecture trips. He joined The Freethinker as an assistant editor in 1898 and was promoted to editor after Foote's death in 1915. Cohen had previously written for various freethought magazines and briefly edited The Truthseeker, which was owned by J.W. Gott. Cohen also replaced Foote as President of the National Secular Society.

CONTENTS

PREFACE

It must be left for those who read the following pages to decide how far this book lives up to its title. That it leaves many aspects of life untouched is quite clear, but there must be a limit to everything, even to the size and scope of a book; moreover, the work does not aim at being an encyclopædia, but only an outline of what may fairly be regarded as the Freethought position. Freethought, again, is too fluid a term to permit its teachings being summarized in a set creed, but it does stand for a certain definite attitude of mind in relation to those problems of life with which thoughtful men and women concern themselves. It is that mental attitude which I aim at depicting.

To those who are not directly concerned with the attack on supernaturalism it may also be a matter of regret that so much of this work is concerned with a criticism of religious beliefs. But that is an accident of the situation. We have not yet reached that stage in affairs when we can afford to let religion alone, and one may readily be excused the suspicion that those who, without believing in it, profess to do so, are more concerned with avoiding a difficult, if not dangerous, subject, than they are with the problem of developing sane and sound methods of thinking. And while some who stand forward as leaders of popular thought fail to do their part in the work of attacking supernaturalistic beliefs, others are perforce compelled to devote more time than they would otherwise to the task. That, in brief, is my apology for concerning myself so largely with religious topics, and leaving almost untouched other fields where the Freethought attitude would prove equally fruitful of results.

After all, it is the mental attitude with which one approaches a problem that really matters. The man or woman who has not learned to set mere authority on one side in dealing with any question will never be more than a mere echo, and what the world needs, now as ever, is not echoes but voices. Information, knowledge, is essential to the helpful consideration of any subject; but all the knowledge in the world will be of very little real help if it is not under the control of a right method. What is called scientific knowledge is, to-day, the commonest of acquisitions, and what most people appear to understand by that is the accumulation of a large number of positive facts which do, indeed, form the raw material of science. But the getting of mere facts is like the getting of money. The value of its accumulation depends upon the use made thereof. It is the power of generalization, the perception and application of principles that is all-important, and to this the grasp of a right method of investigation, the existence of a right mental attitude, is essential.

The world needs knowledge, but still more imperatively it needs the right use of the knowledge that is at its disposal. For this reason I have been mainly concerned in these pages with indicating what I consider to be the right mental attitude with which to approach certain fundamental questions. For, in a world so distracted by conflicting teachings as is ours, the value of a right method is almost incalculable. Scepticism, said Buckle, is not the result, but the condition of progress, and the same may be said of Freethought. The condition of social development is the realization that no institution and no teaching is beyond criticism. Criticism, rejection and modification are the means by which social progress is achieved. It is by criticism of existing ideas and institutions, by the rejection of what is incapable of improvement, and by the modification of what permits of betterment, that we show ourselves worthy of the better traditions of the past, and profitable servants of the present and the future.

C. C.

CHAPTER I
OUTGROWING THE GODS

One of the largest facts in the history of man is religion. If it were otherwise the justification for writing the following pages, and for attempting the proof that, so far as man's history is concerned with religion, it is little better than a colossal blunder, would not be nearly so complete. Moreover, it is a generalization upon which religionists of all classes love to dwell, or even to parade as one of the strongest evidences in their favour; and it is always pleasant to be able to give your opponent all for which he asks—feeling, meanwhile, that you lose nothing in the giving. Universality of belief in religion really proves no more than the universality of telling lies. "All men are liars" is as true, or as false, as "All men are religious." For some men are not liars, and some men are not religious. All the generalization means is that some of both are found in every age and in every country, and that is true whether we are dealing with the liar or with the religious person.

What is ignored is the consideration that while at one stage of culture religious belief is the widest and most embracing of all beliefs it subsequently weakens, not quite in direct proportion to the advance of culture, but yet in such a way that one can say there is an actual relation between a preponderance of the one and a weakening of the other. In very primitive communities gods are born and flourish with all the rank exuberance of a tropical vegetation. In less primitive times their number diminishes, and their sphere of influence becomes more and more sharply defined. The gods are still credited with the ability to do certain things, but there are other things which do somehow get done without them. How that discovery and that division are made need not detain us for the moment, but the fact is patent. Advancing civilization sees the process continued and quickened, nay, that is civilization; for until nature is rid of her "haughty lords" and man realizes that there are at least some natural forces that come within the control of his intelligence, civilization cannot really be said to have commenced. Continued advance sees the gods so diminished in power and so weakened in numbers that their very impotency is apt to breed for them the kind of pity that one feels for a millionaire who becomes a pauper, or for an autocratic monarch reduced to the level of a voteless citizen.

The truth is that all the gods, like their human creators, have in their birth the promise of death. The nature of their birth gives them life, but cannot promise them immortality. However much man commences by worshipping gods, he sooner or later turns his back upon them. Like the biblical deity he may look at his creation and declare it good, but he also resembles this deity in presently feeling the impulse to destroy what he has made. To the products of his mind man can no more give immortality than he can to the work of his hands. In many cases the work of his hands actually outlives that of his mind, for we have to-day the remains of structures that were built in the honour of gods whose very names are forgotten. And to bury his gods is, after all, the only real apology that man can offer for having created them.

This outgrowing of religion is no new thing in human history. Thoughtful observers have always been struck by the mortality among the gods, although their demise has usually been chronicled in terms of exultation by rival worshippers. But here and there a keener observer has brought to bear on the matter a breadth of thought which robbed the phenomenon of its local character and gave it a universal application. Thus, in one of his wonderfully modern dialogues Lucian depicts the Olympian deities discussing, much in the spirit of a modern Church Congress, the prevalence of unbelief among men. The gods are disturbed at finding that men are reaching the stage of either not believing, or not troubling about them. There is a great deal of talk, and finally one of the minor deities treats them to a little plain truth—which appears to be as rare, and as unwelcome in heaven as on earth. He says—I quote from Froude's translation:—

> What other conclusion could they arrive at when they saw the confusion around them? Good men neglected, perishing in penury and slavery, and profligate wretches wealthy, honoured and powerful. Sacrilegious temple robbers undiscovered and unpunished; devotees and saints beaten and crucified. With such phenomena before them, of course men have doubted our existence.... We affect surprise that men who are not fools decline to put their faith in us. We ought rather to be pleased that there is a man left to say his prayers. We are among ourselves with no strangers present. Tell us, then, Zeus, have you ever really taken pains to distinguish between good men and bad? Theseus, not you, destroyed the robbers in Attica. As far as Providence was concerned, Sciron and Pity-O-Campus might have murdered and plundered to the end of time. If Eurystheus had not looked into matters, and sent Hercules upon his

labours little would you have troubled yourself with the
Hydras and Centaurs. Let us be candid. All that we have
really cared for has been a steady altar service. Everything
else has been left to chance. And now men are opening their
eyes. They perceive that whether they pray or don't pray, go
to church or don't go to church, makes no difference to them.
And we are receiving our deserts.

The case could hardly be put more effectively. It is the appeal to
experience with a vengeance, a form of argument of which religionists in
general are very fond. Of course, the argument does not touch the question
of the mere existence of a god, but it does set forth the revolt of awakened
common sense against the worship of a "moral governor of the universe."
We can say of our day, as Lucian said of his, that men are opening their eyes,
and as a consequence the gods are receiving their deserts.

Generally speaking, it is not difficult to see the various steps by which
man outgrew the conception of the government of the world by intelligent
forces. From what we know of primitive thought we may say that at first
the gods dominated all. From the fall of a rain-drop to the movement of a
planet all was the work of gods. Merely to question their power was the
wildest of errors and the gravest of crimes. Bit by bit this vast territory was
reclaimed—a task at the side of which the conquest of the fever-stricken
tropics or the frozen north is mere child's play. It is quite needless to enter
into an elaborate speculation as to the exact steps by which this process
of deanthropomorphization—to use a word of the late John Fiske's—was
accomplished, but one can picture the main line by what we see taking place
at later stages of development. And there is no exception to the rule that
so soon as any group of phenomena is brought within the conception of
law the notion of deity in connection with those phenomena tends to die
out. And the sum of the process is seen in the work of the great law givers
of science, Copernicus, Galileo, Kepler, Newton, Laplace, Lyell, Dalton,
Darwin, etc., who between them have presented us with a universe in which
the conception of deity simply has no place. Apologies apart, the idea of
deity is foreign to the spirit and method of modern science.

In the region of the purely physical sciences this process may be regarded
as complete. In morals and sociology, purely on account of the greater
complexity of the subjects, mystical and semi-supernatural conceptions still
linger, but it is only a question of time for these branches of knowledge to
follow the same course as the physical sciences. In morals we are able to
trace, more or less completely, the development of the moral sense from its
first beginnings in the animal world to its highest developments in man.

What is called the "mystery of morality" simply has no existence to anyone who is not a mystery-monger by profession or inclination. And here, too, the gods have been receiving their deserts. For it is now clear that instead of being a help to morals there has been no greater obstacle to a healthy morality than the play of religious ideas. In the name of God vices have been declared virtues and virtues branded as vices. Belief in God has been an unending source of moral perversion, and it lies upon the face of historical development that an intelligent morality, one that is capable of adapting itself to the changing circumstances of human nature, has only become possible with the breaking down of religious authority.

Exactly the same phenomenon faces us in connection with social life. We have to go back but a little way in human history to come to a time when the existence of a State without a religion would have seemed to people impossible. Much as Christians have quarrelled about other things, they have been in agreement on this point. The historic fight between the established Church and the Nonconformists has never really been for the disestablishment of all religion, and the confining of the State to the discharge of purely secular functions, but mainly as to *which* religion the State shall uphold. To-day, the central issue is whether the State shall teach any religion, whether that does not lie right outside its legitimate functions. And this marks an enormous advance. It is a plain recognition of the truth that the gods have nothing to contribute of any value to the development of our social life. It marks the beginning of the end, and registers the truth that man must be his own saviour here as elsewhere. As in Lucian's day we are beginning to realize that whether we pray or don't pray, go to church or don't go to church, believe in the gods or don't believe in them, makes no real or substantial difference to natural happenings. Now as then we see good men punished and bad ones rewarded, and they who are not fools and have the courage to look facts in the face, decline to put their faith in a deity who is incapable of doing all things right or too careless to exert his power.

It is not that the fight is over, or that there is to-day little need to fight the forces of superstition. If that were so, there would be no need to write what is here written. Much as has been done, there is much yet to do. The revolt against specific beliefs only serves to illustrate a fight that is of much greater importance. For there is little real social gain if one merely exchanges one superstition for another. And, unfortunately, the gentleman who declared that he had given up the errors of the Church of Rome in order to embrace those of the Church of England represents a fairly common type. It is the prevalence of a particular type of mind in society that constitutes a danger, and it is against this that our aim is ultimately directed. Great as is the amount of organized superstition that exists, the amount of unorganized superstition is still greater, and probably more dangerous. One of the revelations of the late war was the evidence it presented of the tremendous amount of raw credulity, of the low type of intelligence that was still current, and the small amount of critical ability the mass of people bring to bear upon life. The legends that gained currency—the army of Russians crossing England, the number of mutilated Belgian babies that were seen, the story of the Germans boiling down their dead to extract the fat, a story that for obscene stupidity beats everything else, the Mons angels, the craze for mascots—all bore witness to the prevalence of a frame of mind that bodes ill for progress.

The truth is, as Sir James Frazer reminds us, that modern society is honeycombed with superstitions that are not in themselves a whit more intellectually respectable than those which dominate the minds of savages. "The smooth surface of cultured society is sapped and mined by superstition." Now and again these hidden mines explode noisily, but the superstition is always there, to be exploited by those who have the wit to use it. From this point of view Christianity is no more than a symptom of a source of great social weakness, a manifestation of a weakness that may find expression in strange and unexpected but always more or less dangerous ways. It is against the prevalence of this type of mind that the Freethinker is really fighting. Freethinkers realize—apparently they are the only ones that do realize—that the creation of a better type of society is finally dependent upon the existence of a sanely educated intelligence, and that will never exist while there are large bodies of people who can persuade themselves that human welfare is in some way dependent upon, or furthered by, practices and beliefs that are not a bit more intellectually respectable than those of the cave men. If Christianity, as a mere system of beliefs, were destroyed, we should only have cleared the way for the final fight. Thousands of generations of superstitious beliefs and practices that have embodied themselves in our laws, our customs, our language, and our institutions, are not to be easily destroyed. It is comparatively simple to destroy a particular manifestation of this disastrous heritage, but the type of mind to which it has given birth is not so easily removed.

The fight is not over, but it is being fought from a new vantage ground, and with better weapons than have ever before been employed. History, anthropology, and psychology have combined to place in the hands of the modern Freethinker more deadly weapons than those of previous generations were able to employ. Before these weapons the defences of the faith crumble like wooden forts before modern artillery. It is no longer a question of debating whether religious beliefs are true. So long as we give a straightforward and honest meaning to those beliefs we know that they are not true. It is, to-day, mainly a question of making plain the nature of the forces which led men and women to regard them as being true. We know that the history of religion is the history of a delusion, and the task of the student is to recover those conditions which gave to this delusion an appearance of truth and reality. That is becoming more and more evident to all serious and informed students of the subject.

The challenge of Freethought to religion constitutes one of the oldest struggles in human history. It must have had its beginning in the first glimmer of doubt concerning a tribal deity which crossed the mind of some more than usually thoughtful savage. Under various forms and in many ways it has gone on ever since. It has had many variations of fortune, often apparently completely crushed, only to rise again stronger and more daring than ever. To-day, Freethought is the accepted mental attitude of a growing number of men and women whose intelligence admits of no question. It has taken a recognized place in the intellectual world, and its hold on the educated intelligence is rapidly increasing. It may well be that in one form or another the antagonism between critical Freethought and accepted teaching, whether secular or religious, will continue as one of the permanent aspects of social conflict. But so far as supernaturalism is concerned the final issue can be no longer in doubt. It is not by one voice or by one movement that supernaturalism is condemned. Its condemnation is written in the best forms of art, science and literature. And that is only another way of saying that it is condemned by life. Freethought holds the future in fee, and nothing but an entire reversal of the order of civilization can force it to forego its claims.

CHAPTER II
LIFE AND MIND

The outstanding feature of what may be called the natural history of associated life is the way in which biologic processes are gradually dominated by psychologic ones. Whatever be the nature of mind, a question that in no way concerns us here, there is no denying the importance of the phenomena that come within that category. To speak of the first beginnings of mind is, in this connection, idle language. In science there are no real beginnings. Things do not begin to be, they simply emerge, and their emergence is as imperceptible as the displacement of night by day, or the development of the chicken from the egg. But whatever the nature of the beginning of mind, its appearance in the evolutionary series marked an event of profound and revolutionary importance. Life received a new impetus, and the struggle for existence a new significance, the importance of which is not, even to-day, generally recognized. The old formulæ might still be used, but they had given to them a new significance. The race was still to the swift and the battle to the strong, but swiftness and strength were manifested in new ways and by new means. Cunning and intelligence began to do what was formerly done without their co-operation. A new force had appeared, arising out of the older forces as chemistry develops from physics and biology from both. And, as we should expect from analogy, we find the new force dominating the older ones, and even bending them to its needs.

Associated life meets us very early in the story of animal existence, and we may assume that it ranks as a genuine "survival quality." It enables some animals to survive the attacks of others that are individually stronger, and it may even be, as has been suggested, that associated life is the normal form, and that solitary animals represent a variation from the normal, or perhaps a case of degeneration. But one result of associated life is that it paves the way for the emergence of mind as an active force in social evolution. In his suggestive and important work on *Mutual Aid*, Kropotkin has well shown how in the animal world the purely biologic form of the struggle for existence is checked and transformed by the factors of mutual aid, association and protection. His illustrations cover a very wide field; they include a great variety of animal forms, and he may fairly claim to have established the proposition that "an instinct has been slowly developed among animals and men in the course of an extremely long evolution ... which has taught animals and men alike the force they can borrow from mutual aid and support, and the joys they can find in social life."

But there is, on the whole, a very sharp limit set to the development of mind in the animal world. One cause of this is the absence of a true "social medium," to use the admirable phrase of that versatile thinker, George Henry Lewes. In the case of man, speech and writing enable him to give to his advances and discoveries a cumulative force such as can never exist in their absence. On that subject more will be said later. At present we may note another very important consequence of the development of mind in evolution. In pre-human, or sub-human society, perfection in the struggle for existence takes the form of the creation or the perfecting of an organic tool. Teeth or claws become stronger or larger, a limb is modified, sight becomes keener, or there is a new effect in coloration. The changes here, it will be observed, are all of an organic kind, they are a part of the animal and are inseparable from it, and they are only transmissible by biologic heredity. And the rate of development is, of necessity, slow.

When we turn to man and note the way in which he overcomes the difficulties of his environment, we find them to be mainly of a different order. His instruments are not personal, in the sense of being a part of his organic structure. We may say they do not belong to him so much as they do to the race; while they are certainly transmitted from generation to generation irrespective of individuals. Instead of achieving conquest of his environment by developing an organic structure, man creates an inorganic tool. In a sense he subdues and moulds the environment to his needs, rather than modifies his structure in order to cope with the environment. Against extremes of temperature he fashions clothing and builds habitations. He discovers fire, probably the most important discovery ever made by mankind. He adds to his strength in defence and attack by inventing weapons. He guards himself from starvation by planting seeds, and so harnesses the productive forces of nature to his needs. He tames animals and so secures living engines of labour. Later, he compensates for his bodily weaknesses by inventing instruments which aid sight, hearing, etc. Inventions are multiplied, methods of locomotion and transportation are discovered, and the difficulties of space and time are steadily minimized. The net result of all this is that as a mere biologic phenomenon man's evolution is checked. The biologic modifications that still go on are of comparatively small importance, except, probably, in the case of evolution against disease. The developments that take place are mainly mental in form and are social in their incidence.

Now if the substantial truth of what has been said be admitted, and I do not see how it can be successfully challenged, there arise one or two considerations of supreme importance. The first of these is that social history becomes more and more a history of social psychology. In social life we are watching the play of social mind expressed through the medium of the individual. The story of civilization is the record of the piling of idea on idea, and the transforming power of the whole on the environment. For tools, from the flint chip of primitive man, down to the finished instrument of the modern mechanic, are all so many products of human mentality. From the primitive dug-out to the Atlantic liner, from the stone spear-head to the modern rifle, in all the inventions of civilized life we are observing the application of mind to the conquest of time, space, and material conditions. Our art, our inventions, our institutions, are all so many illustrations of the power of mind in transforming the environment. A history of civilization, as distinguished from a mere record of biologic growth, is necessarily a history of the growing power of mind. It is the cumulative ideas of the past expressed in inventions and institutions that form the driving power behind the man of to-day. These ideas form the most valuable part of man's heritage, make him what he is, and contain the promise of all that he may become.

So long as we confine ourselves to biologic evolution, the way in which qualities are transmitted is plain. There is no need to go beyond the organism itself. But this heritage of ideas, peculiarly human as it is, requires a "carrier" of an equally unique kind. It is at this point that the significance of what we have called the "social medium" emerges. The full significance of this was first seen by G. H. Lewes.[1] Writing so far back as 1879 he said:—

> The distinguishing character of human psychology is that to the three great factors, organism, external medium, and heredity; it adds a fourth, namely, the relation to a social medium, with its product, the general mind.... While the mental functions are products of the individual organism, the product, mind, is more than an individual product. Like its great instrument language, it is at once individual and social. Each man speaks in virtue of the functions of vocal expression, but also in virtue of the social need of communication. The words spoken are not his creation, yet he, too, must appropriate them by what may be called a creative process before he can understand them. What his tribe speaks he repeats; but he does not simply echo their words, he rethinks them. In the same way he adopts their experiences when he assimilates them to his own.... Further,

the experiences come and go; they correct, enlarge, and destroy one another, leaving behind them a certain residual store, which condensed in intuitions and formulated in principles, direct and modify all future experiences.... Men living in groups co-operate like the organs in an organism. Their actions have a common impulse to a common end. Their desires and opinions bear the common stamp of an impersonal direction. Much of their life is common to all. The roads, market-places and temples are for each and all. Customs arise and are formulated in laws, the restraint of all.... Each generation is born in this social medium, and has to adapt itself to the established forms.... A nation, a tribe, a sect is the medium of the individual mind, as a sea, a river, or a pond, is the medium of a fish.[2]

Biologically, what man inherits is capacity for acquisition. But what he shall acquire, the direction in which his native capacity shall express itself, is a matter over which biologic forces have no control. This is determined by society and social life. Given quite equal capacity in two individuals, the output will be very different if one is brought up in a remote Spanish village and the other in Paris or London. Whether a man shouts long live King George or long live the Kaiser is mainly a question of social surroundings, and but very little one of difference in native capacity. The child of parents living in the highest civilized society, if taken away while very young and brought up amid a people in a very primitive state of culture, would, on reaching maturity, differ but little from the people around him. He would think the thoughts that were common to the society in which he was living as he would speak their language and wear their dress. Had Shakespeare been born among savages he could never have written *Hamlet*. For the work of the genius, as for that of the average man, society must provide the materials in the shape of language, ideas, institutions, and the thousand and one other things that go to make up the life of a group, and which may be seen reflected in the life of the individual. Suppose, says Dr. McDougall:—

that throughout the period of half a century every child born to English parents was at once exchanged (by the power of a magician's wand) for an infant of the French, or other, European nation. Soon after the close of this period the English nation would be composed of individuals of French extraction, and the French of individuals of English extraction. It is, I think, clear that, in spite of this complete exchange of innate characters between the two nations, there would be but little immediate change of national characteristics. The

French people would still speak French, and the English would speak English, with all the local diversities to which we are accustomed and without perceptible change of pronunciation. The religion of the French would still be predominantly Roman Catholic, and the English people would still present the same diversity of Protestant creeds. The course of political institutions would have suffered no profound change, the customs and habits of the two peoples would exhibit only such changes as might be attributed to the lapse of time, though an acute observer might notice an appreciable approximation of the two peoples towards one another in all these respects. The inhabitant of France would still be a Frenchman and the inhabitant of England an Englishman to all outward seeming, save that the physical appearance of the two peoples would be transposed. And we may go even further and assert that the same would hold good if a similar exchange of infants were effected between the English and any other less closely allied nation, say the Turks or the Japanese.[3]

The products of human capacity are the material of which civilization is built; these products constitute the inheritance which one generation receives from another. Whether this inheritance be large or small, simple or complex, it is the chief determinant which shapes the personality of each individual. What each has by biological heredity is a given structure, that is, capacity. But the direction of that capacity, the command it enables one to acquire over his environment, is in turn determined by the society into which he happens to be born.

It has already been said that the materials of civilization, whether they be tools, or institutions, or inventions, or discoveries, or religious or ethical teachings, are facts that can be directly described as psychological. An institution—the Church, the Crown, the Magistracy—is not transmitted as a building or as so many sheets of paper, but as an idea or as a set of ideas. A piece of machinery is, in the same way, a mental fact, and is a physical one in only a subordinate sense. And if this be admitted, we reach the further truth that the environment to which man has to adapt himself is essentially, so far as it is a social environment, psychological. Not alone are the outward marks of social life—the houses in which man lives, the machines he uses to do his bidding—products of his mental activity, but the more important features of his environment, to which he must adapt himself, and which so largely shape his character and determine his conduct, are of a wholly psychological character. In any society that is at all distinct from the animal, there exist a number of beliefs, ideas and institutions, traditions, and, in a later stage, a literature which play a very important part in determining the direction of man's mind. With increasing civilization, and the development of better means of intercourse, any single society finds itself brought into touch and under the influence of other social groups. The whole of these influences constitute a force which, surrounding an individual at birth, inevitably shapes character in this or that direction. They dominate the physical aspect of life, and represent the determining forces of social growth. Eliminate the psychological forces of life and you eliminate all that can be properly called civilization. It is wholly the transforming power of mind on the environment that creates civilization, and it is only by a steady grasp of this fact that civilization can be properly understood.

I have pointed out a distinction between biological and social, or psychological, heredity. But there is one instance in which the two agree. This is that we can only understand a thing by its history. We may catalogue the existing peculiarities of an animal form with no other material than that of the organism before us, but thoroughly to understand it we must know its history. Similarly, existing institutions may have their justification in the present, but the causes of their existence lie buried in the past. A king may to-day be honoured on account of his personal worth, but the reason why there is a king to be honoured carries us back to that state of culture in which the primitive priest and magic worker inspires fear and awe. When we ring bells to call people to church we perpetuate the fact that our ancestors rang them to drive away evil spirits. We wear black at a funeral because our primitive ancestors wished to hide themselves from the dead man's ghost. We strew flowers on a grave because food and other things were once buried with the dead so that their spirits might accompany the dead to the next world. In short, with all human customs we are forced, if we wish to know the reason for their present existence, to seek it in the ideas that have dominated the minds of previous generations.[4]

No one who has studied, in even a cursory manner, the development of our social institutions can avoid recognition of the profound influence exerted by the primitive conceptions of life, death, and of the character of natural forces. Every one of our social institutions was born in the shadow of superstition, and superstition acts as a powerful force in determining the form they assume. Sir Henry Maine has shown to what a large extent the laws of inheritance are bound up with ancestor worship.[5] Spencer has done the same service for nearly all our institutions,[6] and Mr. Elton says that "the oldest customs of inheritance in England and Germany were, in their beginnings, connected with a domestic religion, and based upon a worship of ancestral spirits of which the hearthplace was essentially the altar."[7]

The same truth meets us in the study of almost any institution. In fact, it is not long before one who *thinks* evolution, instead of merely knowing its formulæ, begins to realize the truth of the saying by a German sociologist that in dealing with social institutions we are concerned with the "mental creations of aggregates." They are dependent upon the persistence of a set of ideas, and so long as these ideas are unshaken they are substantially indestructible. To remove them the ideas upon which they rest must be shaken and robbed of their authority. That is the reason why at all times the fight for reform so largely resolves itself into a contest of ideas. Motives of self-interest may enter into the defence of an institution, and in some case may be responsible for the attempt to plant an institution where it does not already exist, but in the main institutions persist because of their harmony with a frame of mind that is favourable to their being.

A great deal of criticism has been directed against the conclusion of Buckle that improvement in the state of mankind has chiefly resulted from an improvement in the intellectual outlook. And yet when stated with the necessary qualifications the generalization is as sound as it can well be. Certainly, the belief held in some quarters, and stated with an air of scientific precision, that the material environment is the active force which is ever urging to new mental development will not fit the facts; for, as we have seen, the environment to which human nature must adapt itself is mainly mental in character, that is, it is made up in an increasing measure of the products of man's own mental activity. The theory of the sentimental religionist that the evil in the world results from the wickedness of man, or, as he is fond of putting it, from the hardness of man's heart, is grotesque in its ineffectiveness. Soft heads have far more to do with the evil in the world than have hard hearts. Indeed, one of the standing difficulties of the orthodox moralist is, not to explain the deeds of evil men, which explain themselves, but to account for the harm done by "good" men, and often as a consequence of their goodness. The moral monster is a rarity, and evil is rarely the outcome of a clear perception of its nature and a deliberate resolve to pursue it. Paradoxical as it may sound, it demands a measure of moral strength to do wrong, consciously and deliberately, which the average man or woman does not possess. And the world has never found it a matter of great difficulty to deal with its "bad" characters; it is the "good" ones that present it with a constant problem.

The point is worth stressing, and we may do it from more than one point of view. We may take, first of all, the familiar illustration of religious persecution, as exemplified in the quarrels of Catholics and Protestants. On the ground of moral distinction no line could be drawn between the two parties. Each shuddered at the persecution inflicted by the other, and each regarded the teachings of the other with the same degree of moral aversion. And it has often been noted that the men who administered so infamous an institution as the Inquisition were not, in even the majority of cases, bad men.[8] A few may have had interested motives, but it would have been impossible to have maintained so brutal an institution in the absence of a general conviction of its rightness. In private life those who could deliver men, women, and even children over to torture were not worse husbands or parents than others. Such differences as existed cannot be attributed to a lack of moral endeavour, or to a difference of "moral temperament." It was a difference of intellectual outlook, and given certain religious convictions persecution became a religious necessity. The moral output was poor because the intellectual standpoint was a wrong one.

If we could once get over the delusion of thinking of human nature as being fundamentally different five hundred years ago from what it is to-day, we should escape a great many fallacies that are prevalent. The changes that have taken place in human nature during the historic period are so slight as to be practically negligible. The motives that animate men and women to-day are the motives that animated men and women a thousand or two thousand years ago. The change is in the direction and form of their manifestation only, and it is in the light of the human nature around us that we must study and interpret the human nature that has gone before us. From that point of view we may safely conclude that bad institutions were kept in being in the past for the same reason that they are kept alive to-day. The majority must be blind to their badness; and in any case it is a general perception of their badness which leads to their destruction.

The subject of crime illustrates the same point. Against crime as such, society is as set as ever. But our attitude toward the causation and cure of crime, and, above all, to the treatment of the criminal, has undergone a profound alteration. And the change that has taken place here has been away from the Christian conception which brutalized the world for so long, towards the point of view taken up by the ancient Greeks, that wrong doing is the outcome of ignorance. Expressed in the modern manner we should say that crime is the result of an undeveloped nature, or of a pathological one, or of a reversion to an earlier predatory type, or the result of any or all of these factors in combination with defective social conditions. But this is only another way of saying that we have exchanged the old, brutal, and ineffective methods for more humane and effective ones because we look at the problem of crime from a different intellectual angle. A more exact knowledge of the causation of crime has led us to a more sensible and a more humane treatment of the criminal. And this, not alone in his own behalf, but in the interests of the society in which he lives. We may put it broadly that improvement comes from an enlightened way of looking at things. Common observation shows that people will go on tolerating forms of brutality, year after year, without the least sense of their wrongness. Familiarity, and the absence of any impetus to examine current practice from a new point of view seem to account for this. In the seventeenth century the same people who could watch, without any apparent hostility, the torture of an old woman on the fantastic charge of intercourse with Satan, had their feelings outraged by hearing a secular song on Sunday. Imprisonment for "blasphemy," once regarded as a duty, has now become ridiculous to all reasonable people. At one and the same time, a little more than a hundred years ago in this country, the same people who could denounce cock-fighting on account of its brutality, could watch unmoved the murdering of little children in the factories of Lancashire. Not so long ago men in this country fought duels under a sense of moral compulsion, and the practice was only abandoned when a changed point of view made people realize the absurdity of trying to settle the justice of a cause by determining which of two people were the most proficient with sword or pistol. We have a continuation of the same absurdity in those larger duels fought by nations where the old verbal absurdities still retain their full force, and where we actually add another absurdity by retaining a number of professional duellists who must be ready to embark on a duel whether they have any personal feeling in the matter or not. And it seems fairly safe to say that when it is realized that the duel between nations as a means of settling differences is not a bit more intellectually respectable than was the ancient duello we shall not be far removed from seeing the end of one of the greatest dangers to which modern society is exposed.

Examples might be multiplied indefinitely, but enough has been said to show what small reason there is for assuming that changes in institutions are brought about by the operation of some occult moral sense. It is the enlightenment of the moral sense by the growth of new ideas, by the impact of new knowledge leading to a revaluation of things that is mainly responsible for the change. The question of whether a man should or should not be burned for a difference in religious belief was never one that could be settled by weighing up the moral qualities of the two parties in the dispute. All the moral judgment that has ever existed, even if combined in the person of a single individual could never decide that issue. It was entirely a question of acquiring a new point of view from which to examine the subject. Until that was done the whole force of the moral sense was on the side of the persecutor. To put the matter paradoxically, the better the man the worse persecutor he became. It was mental enlightenment that was needed, not moral enthusiasm.

The question of progress thus becomes, in all directions, one of the impact of new ideas, in an environment suitable to their reception and growth. A society shut in on itself is always comparatively unprogressive, and but for the movement of classes within it would be completely so. The more closely the history of civilization is studied the more clearly does that fact emerge. Civilization is a synthetic movement, and there can be no synthesis in the absence of dissolution and resolution.

A fight of old ideas against new ones, a contest of clashing culture levels, a struggle to get old things looked at from a new point of view, these are the features that characterize all efforts after reform. It was said by some of the eighteenth century philosophers that society was held together by agreement in a bond. That is not quite correct. The truth is that society is held together, as is any phase of social life, by a bond of agreement. The agreement is not of the conscious, documentary order, but it is there, and it consists in sharing a common life created and maintained by having a common tradition, and a common stock of ideas and ideals. It is this that makes a man a member of one social group rather than of another—Chinese, American, French, German, or Choctaw. There is no discriminating feature in what is called the economic needs of people. The economic needs of human beings—food, clothing, and shelter, are of the same order the world over. And certainly the fact of a Chinaman sharing in the economic life of Britain, or an Englishman sharing in the economic life of China, would not entitle either to be called genuine members of the group in which he happened to be living. Membership only begins to be when those belonging to a group share in a common mental outfit. Even within a society, and in relation to certain social groups, one can see illustrations of the same principle. A man is not really a member of a society of artists, lawyers, or doctors merely by payment of an annual subscription. He is that only when he becomes a participant in the mental life of the group.[9] It is this common stock of mental facts which lies at the root of all collective ideas—an army, a Church, or a nation. And ever the fight is by way of attack and defence of the psychologic fact.[10]

To do the Churches and other vested interests justice, they have never lost sight of this truth, and it would have been better for the race had others been equally alive to its importance. The Churches have never ceased to fight for the control of those public organs that make for the formation of opinion. Their struggle to control the press, the platform, and the school means just this. Whatever they may have taught, self-interest forced upon them recognition of the truth that it was what men thought about things that mattered. They have always opposed the introduction of new ideas, and have fought for the retention of old ones. It was a necessity of their existence. It was also an admission of the truth that in order for reform to become a fact the power of traditional ideas must be broken. Man is what he thinks, is far nearer the truth than the once famous saying, "Man is what he eats." As a member of a social group man is dominated by his ideas of things, and any movement of reform must take cognisance of that fact if it is to cherish reasonable hopes of success.

CHAPTER III
WHAT IS FREETHOUGHT?

Freedom of thought and freedom of speech stand to each other as the two halves of a pair of scissors. Without freedom of speech freedom of thought is robbed of the better part of its utility, even if its existence is not threatened. The one reacts on the other. As thought provides the material for speech, so, in turn, it deteriorates when it is denied expression. Speech is, in fact, one of the great factors in human progress. It is that which enables one generation to hand on to another the discoveries made, the inventions produced, the thoughts achieved, and so gives a degree of fixity to the progress attained. For progress, while expressed through the individual, is achieved by the race. Individually, the man of to-day is not strikingly superior in form or capacity to the man of five or ten thousand years ago. But he knows more, can achieve more, and is in that sense stronger than was his ancestors. He is the heir of the ages, not as a figure of speech, but as the most sober of facts. He inherits what previous generations have acquired; the schoolboy of to-day starts with a capital of inherited knowledge that would have been an outfit for a philosopher a few thousand years ago.

It is this that makes speech of so great importance to the fact of progress. Without speech, written or verbal, it would be impossible to conserve the products of human achievement. Each generation would have to start where its predecessor commenced, and it would finish at about the same point. It would be the fable of Sisyphus illustrated in the passing of each generation of human beings.

But speech implies communication. There is not very much pleasure in speaking to oneself. Even the man who apologised for the practice on the ground that he liked to address a sensible assembly would soon grow tired of so restricted an audience. The function of speech is to transmit ideas, and it follows, therefore, that every embargo on the free exchange of ideas, every obstacle to complete freedom of speech, is a direct threat to the well-being of civilisation. As Milton could say that a good book "is the precious life-blood of a master spirit, embalmed and treasured up to a life beyond life," and that "he who destroys a good book kills reason itself," so we may say that he who strikes at freedom of thought and speech is aiming a blow at the very heart of human betterment.

In theory, the truth of what has been said would be readily admitted, but in practice it has met, and still meets, with a vigorous opposition. Governments have exhausted their powers to prevent freedom of intercourse between peoples, and every Church and chapel has used its best endeavours to the same end. Even to-day, when all are ready to pay lip-homage to freedom of thought, the obstacles in the way of a genuine freedom are still very great. Under the best possible conditions there will probably always be some coercion of opinion, if only of that unconscious kind which society as a whole exerts upon its individual members. But to this we have to add the coercion that is consciously exerted to secure the formation of particular opinions, and which has the dual effect of inducing dissimulation in some and impotency in others. Quite ignorantly parents commence the work when they force upon children their own views of religion and inculcate an exaggerated respect for authority. They create an initial bias that is in only too many cases fatal to real independence of thought. Social pressure continues what a mistaken early training has commenced. When opinions are made the test of "good form," and one's social standing partly determined by the kind of opinions that one holds, there is developed on the one side hypocrisy, and on the other, because certain opinions are banned, thought in general is unhealthily freed from the sobering influence of enlightened criticism.[11]

To-day the legal prohibition of religious dissent is practically ineffective, and is certainly far less demoralizing than the pressure that is exerted socially and unofficially. In all probability this has always been the case. For legal persecution must be open. Part of its purpose is publicity, and that in itself is apt to rouse hostility. Against open, legal persecution a man will make a stand, or if he gives way to the force arrayed against him may do so with no feeling of personal degradation. But the conformity that is secured by a threat of social boycott, the freedom of speech that is prevented by choking the avenues of intellectual intercourse, is far more deadly in its consequences, and far more demoralizing in its influence on character. To give way, as thousands do, not to the open application of force, which carries no greater personal reflection than does the soldier's surrender to superior numbers, but to the dread of financial loss, to the fear of losing a social status, that one may inwardly despise even while in the act of securing it, or from fear of offending those whom we may feel are not worthy of our respect, these are the things that cannot be done without eating into one's sense of self-respect, and inflicting upon one's character an irreparable injury.

On this matter more will be said later. For the present I am concerned with the sense in which we are using the word "Freethought." Fortunately, little time need be wasted in discussing the once popular retort to the Freethinker that if the principle of determinism be accepted "free" thought is impossible. It is surprising that such an argument should ever have secured a vogue, and is only now interesting as an indication of the mentality of the defender of orthodox religion. Certainly no one who properly understands the meaning of the word would use such an argument. At best it is taking a word from sociology, a sphere in which the meaning is quite clear and intelligible, and applying it in the region of physical science where it has not, and is not intended to have, any meaning at all. In physical science a thing is what it does, and the business of science is to note the doings of forces and masses, their actions and reactions, and express them in terms of natural "law." From the point of view of physical science a thing is neither free nor unfree, and to discuss natural happenings in terms of freedom or bondage is equal to discussing smell in terms of sight or colour in terms of smell. But applied in a legitimate way the word "free" is not only justifiable, it is indispensible. The confusion arises when we take a word from a department in which its meaning is quite clear and apply it in a region where it has no application whatever.

Applied to opinion "Free" has the same origin and the same application as the expressions "a free man," or a "free State," or "a free people." Taking either of these expressions it is plain that they could have originated only in a state of affairs where some people are "free," and some are living in a state of bondage or restraint. There is no need to trace the history of this since so much is implied in the word itself. A free State is one in which those belonging to it determine their own laws without being coerced by an outside power. A free man is one who is permitted to act as his own nature prompts. The word "free" implies nothing as to the nature of moral or mental causation, that is a question of a wholly different order. The free man exists over against the one who is not free, the free State over against one that is held in some degree of subjection to another State. There is no other meaning to the word, and that meaning is quite clear and definite.

Now Freethought has a precisely similar significance. It says nothing as to the nature of thought, the origin of thought, or the laws of thought. With none of these questions is it vitally concerned. It simply asserts that there are conditions under which thought is not "free," that is, where it is coerced to a foregone conclusion, and that these conditions are fatal to thought in its higher and more valuable aspects. Freethought is that form of thinking that proceeds along lines of its own determining, rather than along lines that are laid down by authority. In actual practice it is immediately concerned with the expression of opinion rather than with its formation, since no authority can prevent the formation of opinion in any mind that is at all independent in its movements and forms opinions on the basis of observed facts and adequate reasoning. But its chief and primary significance lies in its repudiation of the right of authority to say what form the expression of opinion shall take. And it is also clear that such a term as "Freethought" could only have come into general use and prominence in a society in which the free circulation of opinion was more or less impeded.

It thus becomes specially significant that, merely as a matter of history, the first active manifestation of Freethought should have occurred in connection with a revolt against religious teaching and authority. This was no accident, but was rather a case of necessity. For, in the first place, there is no other subject in which pure authority plays so large a part as it does in religion. All churches and all priesthoods, ancient and modern, fall back upon the principle of pure authority as a final method of enforcing their hold upon the people. That, it may be noted in passing, is one of the chief reasons why in all ages governments have found religion one of the most serviceable agencies in maintaining their sway. Secondly, there seems to have been from the very earliest times a radically different frame of mind in the approach to secular and religious matters. So far as one can see there appears to be, even in primitive societies, no very strong opposition to the free discussion of matters that are of a purely secular nature. Questions of ways and means concerning these are freely debated among savage tribes, and in all discussion differences of opinion must be taken for granted. It is when we approach religious subjects that a difference is seen. Here the main concern is to determine the will of the gods, and all reasoning is thus out of place, if not a positive danger. The only thing is to discover "God's will," and when we have his, or his will given in "sacred" books the embargo on free thinking is complete. This feature continues to the end. We do not even to-day discuss religious matters in the same open spirit in which secular matters are debated. There is a bated breath, a timidity of criticism in discussing religious subjects that does not appear when we are discussing secular topics. With the thoroughly religious man it is solely a question of what God wishes him to do. In religion this affords the only latitude for discussion, and even that disappears largely when the will of God is placed before the people in the shape of "revealed" writings. Fortunately for the world "inspired" writings have never been so clearly penned as to leave no room for doubt as to what they actually meant. Clarity of meaning has never been one of the qualities of divine authorship.

In this connection it is significant that the first form of democratic government of which we have any clear record should have been in freethinking, sceptical Greece. Equally notable is it that in both Rome and Greece the measure of mental toleration was greater than it has ever been in other countries before or since. In Rome to the very end of the Pagan domination there existed no legislation against opinions, as such. The holders of certain opinions might find themselves in uncomfortable positions now and then, but action against them had to rest on some ground other than that which was afterwards known as heresy. There existed no law in the Roman Empire against freedom of opinion, and those who are familiar with Mr. H. C. Lea's classic, *History of the Inquisition*, will recall his account of the various tactics adopted by the Christian Church to introduce measures that would accustom the public mind to legislation which should establish the principle of persecution for opinion.[12] In the end the Church succeeded in effecting this, and its success was registered in the almost unbelievable degradation of the human intellect which was exhibited in the Christian world for centuries. So complete was this demoralization that more than a thousand years later we find men announcing as a most daring principle a demand for freedom of discussion which in old Greece and Rome was never officially questioned. Christianity not merely killed freedom wherever it established itself, but it came very near killing even the memory of it.

It was, therefore, inevitable that in the western world Freethought should come into prominence in relation to the Christian religion and its claims. In the Christian Church there existed an organization which not alone worked with the avowed intention of determining what men should think, but finally proceeded to what was, perhaps, the logical conclusion, to say what they should not think. No greater tyranny than the Christian Church has ever existed. And this applies, not to the Roman Church alone, but to every Church within the limit of its opportunities. In the name and in the interests of religion the Christian Church took some of the worst passions of men and consecrated them. The killing of heretics became one of the most solemn duties and it was urged upon secular rulers as such. The greatest instrument of oppression ever formed, the Inquisition, was fashioned for no other purpose than to root out opinions that were obnoxious to the Church. It would have been bad enough had the attempts of the Church to control opinion been limited to religion. But that was not the case. It aimed at taking under its control all sorts of teaching on all sorts of subjects. Nothing would have surprised an inhabitant of ancient Rome more, could he have revisited the earth some dozen centuries after the establishment of Christianity, than to have found men being punished for criticising doctrines that were in his day openly laughed at. And nothing could have given an ancient Athenian greater cause for wonder than to have found men being imprisoned and burned for teaching cosmical theories that were being debated in the schools of Athens two thousand years before. Well might they have wondered what had happened to the world, and well might they have come to the conclusion that it had been overtaken by an attack of universal insanity. And the explanation would not have been so very wide of the truth.

In this matter of suppression of freedom of thinking there was little to choose between the Churches. Each aimed at controlling the thought of mankind, each was equally intolerant of any variation from the set line, and each employed the same weapon of coercion so far as circumstances permitted. At most the Protestant Churches substituted a dead book for a living Church, and in the end it may be questioned, when all allowance is made for the changed circumstances in which Protestantism operated, whether the rule of the new Church was not more disastrous than the older one. It had certainly less excuse for its intolerance. The Roman Catholic Church might urge that it never claimed to stand for freedom of opinion, and whatever its sins it was so far free from the offence of hypocrisy. But the Protestant Churches could set up no such plea; they professed to stand on freedom of conscience. And they thus added the quality of inconsistency and hypocrisy to an offence that was already grave enough in itself.

But whatever opinion one may have on that point, it is certain that in practice the Protestant leaders were as opposed to freedom of thought as were the Roman Catholics. And Protestant bigotry left a mark on European history that deserves special recognition. For the first time it made the profession of Christianity a definite part of the law of the secular State.[13] Hitherto there had been no law in any of the European States which made a profession of Christianity necessary. There had been plenty of persecutions of non-Christians, and the consequences of a rejection of Christianity, if one lived in a Christian State, were serious enough. But when the secular State punished the heretic it was a manifestation of good will towards the Church and not the expression of a legal enactment. It was the direct influence of the Church on the State. Church and State were legally distinct during the mediæval period, however closely they may have been allied in practice. With the arrival of Protestantism and the backing of the reformed religion given by certain of the Princes, the machinery of intolerance, so to speak, was taken over by the State and became one of its functions. It became as much the duty of the secular officials to extirpate heresy, to secure uniformity of religious belief as it was to the interest of the Church to see that it was destroyed. Up to that time it was the aim of the Church to make the State one of its departments. It had never legally succeeded in doing this, but it was not for the Roman Church to sink to the subordinate position of becoming a department of the State. It was left for Protestantism to make the Church a branch of the State and to give religious bigotry the full sanction of secular law.

Neither with Catholic nor Protestant could there be, therefore, any relaxation in the opposition offered to independent thinking. That still remained the cardinal offence to the religious mind. In the name of religion Protestants opposed the physics of Newton as bitterly as Catholics opposed the physics of Galileo. The geology of Hutton and Lyell, the chemistry of Boyle and Dalton, the biology of Von Baer, Lamarck and Darwin, with almost any other branch of science that one cares to select, tell the same tale. And when the desire for reform took a social turn there was the same influence to be fought. For while the Roman Catholic laid the chief insistence on obedience to the Church, the Protestant laid as strong insistence on obedience to the State, and made disobedience to its orders a matter of almost religious revolt. The whole force of religion was thus used to induce contentment with the existing order, instead of to the creation of an intelligent discontent which would lead to continuous improvement. In view of these circumstances it is not surprising that the word "Freethought" should have lost in actual use its more general significance of a denial of the place of mere authority in matters of opinion, and have acquired a more definite and precise connotation. It could not, of course, lose its general meaning, but it gained a special application and became properly associated with a definitely anti-theological attitude. The growth in this direction was gradual but inevitable. When the term first came into general use, about the end of the seventeenth century, it was mainly used with reference to those deists who were then attacking Christianity. In that sense it continued to be used for some time. But as Deism lost ground, thanks partly to the Christian attack, the clear and logical issue between Theism and Atheism became apparent, with the result that the definite anti-religious character of "Freethought" became firmly established. And to-day it is mere affectation or timidity to pretend that the word has any other vital significance. To say that a man is a Freethinker is to give, to ninety-nine people out of a hundred, the impression that he is anti-religious. And in this direction the popular sense of the word discloses what has been its important historic function. Historically, the chief stronghold of mere authority has been religion. In science and in sociology, as well as in connection with supernaturalism proper, every movement in the direction of the free exercise of the intellect has met with the unceasing opposition of religion. That has always been at once the symbol and the instrument of oppression. To attack religion has been to attack the enemy in his capital. All else has been matter of outpost skirmishing.

I have apparently gone a long way round to get at the meaning of the word "Freethought," but it was necessary. For it is of very little use, in the case of an important word that has stood and stands for the name of a movement, to go to a dictionary, or to appeal to etymology. The latter has often a mere antiquarian interest, and the former merely registers current meanings, it does not make them. The use of a word must ultimately be determined by the ideas it conveys to those who hear it. And from what has been said the meaning of this particular word should be fairly clear. While standing historically for a reasoned protest against the imposition of opinion by authority, and, negatively, against such artificial conditions as prevent the free circulation of opinion, it to-day stands actually for a definitely anti-religious mental attitude. And this is what one would naturally expect. Protests, after all, are protests against something in the concrete, even though they may embody the affirmation of an abstract principle. And nowadays the principle of pure authority has so few defenders that it would be sheer waste of time, unless the protest embodied a definite attitude with regard to specific questions. We may, then, put it that to us "Freethought" stands for a reasoned and definite opposition to all forms of supernaturalism, it claims the right to subject all religious beliefs to the test of reason, and further claims that when so tested they break down hopelessly. It is from this point of view that these pages are written, and the warranty for so defining it should be apparent from what has been said in this and the preceding chapter.

CHAPTER IV
REBELLION AND REFORM

Rebellion and reform are not exactly twins, but they are very closely related. For while all rebellion is not reform, yet in the widest sense of the word, there is no reform without rebellion. To fight for reform is to rebel against the existing order and is part of the eternal and fundamentally healthful struggle of the new against the old, and of the living present against the dead past. The rebel is thus at once a public danger and a benefactor. He threatens the existing order, but it is in the name of a larger and better social life. And because of this it is his usual lot to be crucified when living and deified when dead. So it has always been, so in its main features will it always be. If contemporaries were to recognize the reformer as such, they would destroy his essential function by making it useless. Improvement would become an automatic process that would perfect itself without opposition. As it is, the function of the rebel is to act as an explosive force, and no society of average human beings likes explosions. They are noisy, and they are dangerous. For the reformer to complain at not being hailed as a deliverer is for him to mistake his part and place in social evolution.

The rebel and the reformer is, again, always in minority. That follows from what has already been said. It follows, too, from what we know of development in general. Darwinism rests on the supreme importance of the minority. It is an odd variation here and there that acts as the starting point for a new species—and it has against it the swamping influence of the rest of its kind that treads the old biological line. Nature's choicest variations are of necessity with the few, and when that variation has established itself and become normal another has to appear before a new start can be made.

Whether we take biology or psychology the same condition appears. A new idea occurs to an individual and it is as strictly a variation from the normal as anything that occurs in the animal world. The idea may form the starting point of a new theory, or perhaps of a new social order. But to establish itself, to become the characteristic property of the group, it must run the gamut of persecution and the risk of suppression. And suppressed it often is—for a time. It is an idle maxim which teaches that truth always conquers, if by that is implied that it does so at once. That is not the truth.

Lies have been victorious over and over again. The Roman Catholic Church, one of the greatest lies in the history of the human race, stood the conqueror for many centuries. The teaching of the rotundity of the earth and its revolution round the sun was suppressed for hundreds of years until it was revived in the 16th century. In the long run truth does emerge, but a lie may have a terribly lengthy innings. For the lie is accepted by the many, while the truth is seen only by the few. But it is the few to whom we turn when we look over the names of those who have made the world what is it. All the benefits to society come from the few, and society crucifies them to show its gratitude. One may put it that society lives on the usual, but flourishes on account of the exception.

Now there is something extremely significant in the Christian religion tracing all the disasters of mankind to a primal act of disobedience. It is a fact which discloses in a flash the chief social function of religion in general and of Christianity in particular. Man's duty is summed up in the one word obedience, and the function of the (religiously) good man is to obey the commands of God, as that of the good citizen is to obey the commands of government. The two commands meet and supplement each other with the mutual advantage which results from the adjustment of the upper and lower jaws of a hyena. And it explains why the powers that be have always favoured the claims of religion. It enabled them to rally to their aid the tremendous and stupefying aid of religion and to place rebellion to their orders on the same level as rebellion against God. In Christian theology Satan is the arch-rebel; hell is full of rebellious angels and disobedient men and women. Heaven is reserved for the timid, the tame, the obedient, the sheep-like. When the Christ of the Gospels divides the people into goats and sheep, it is the former that go to hell, and the latter to heaven. The Church has not a rebel in its calendar, although it has not a few rogues and many fools. To the Church rebellion is always a sin, save on those rare occasions when revolt is ordered in the interests of the Church itself. In Greek mythology Prometheus steals fire from heaven for the benefit of man and suffers in consequence. The myth symbolizes the fact. Always the man has had to win knowledge and happiness in the teeth of opposition from the gods. Always the race has owed its progress to the daring of the rebel or of the rebellious few.

Often the Freethinker is denounced because he is destructive or dangerous. What other is he expected to be? And would he be of much use if he were otherwise?? I would go further and say that he is the most destructive of all agencies because he is so intimately concerned with the handling of the most destructive of weapons—ideas. We waste a good deal of time in denouncing certain people as dangerous when they are in reality comparatively harmless. A man throws a bomb, or breaks into a house, or robs one of a purse, and a judge solemnly denounces him as a most "dangerous member of society." It is all wrong. These are comparatively harmless individuals. One man throws a bomb, kills a few people, damages some property, and there the matter ends. Another man comes along and drops instead of a bomb a few ideas, and the whole country is in a state of eruption. Charles Peace pursues a career of piety and crime, gets himself comfortably and religiously hanged, and society congratulates itself on having got rid of a dangerous person, and then forgets all about it. Karl Marx visits England, prowls round London studying the life of rich and poor, and drops *Das Kapital* on us. A quiet and outwardly inoffensive individual, one who never gave the police a moment's anxiety, spends years studying earthworms, and flowers, and horses and cats, and all sorts of moving things and presents society with *The Origin of Species*. Organized society found itself able to easily guard itself against the attacks of men such as Charles Peace, it may with impunity extend its hospitality to the thrower of bombs, or robber of houses, but by what means can it protect itself against the "peaceful" Marx or the "harmless" Darwin? No society can afford to ignore in its midst a score of original or independent thinkers, or if society does ignore them they will not for long ignore society. The thinker is really destructive. He destroys because he creates; he creates because he destroys. The one is the obverse of the other.

I am not making idle play with the word "destruction." It is literally true that in human society the most destructive and the most coercive forces at work are ideas. They strike at established institutions and demand either their modification or their removal. That is why the emergence of a new idea is always an event of social significance. Whether it be a good idea or a bad one will not affect the truth of this statement. For over four years our political mediocrities and muddle headed militarists were acting as though the real problem before them was to establish the superiority of one armed group of men over another group. That was really a simple matter. The important issue which society had to face was the ideas that the shock of the war must give rise to. Thinkers saw this; but thinkers do not get the public ear either as politicians or militarists. And now events are driving home the lesson. The ideas of Bolshevism and Sinn Feinism proved far more "dangerous" than the German armies. The Allied forces could handle the one, but they were powerless before the other. It is not a question of whether these particular ideas are good or bad, or whether we approve or disapprove of them, but entirely one that, being ideas, they represent a far more "destructive" power than either bomb or gun. They are at once the forces that act as the cement of society and those that may hurl it into chaotic fragments.

Whether an idea will survive or not must, in the end, be determined by circumstances, but in itself a new idea may be taken as the mental analogue of the variation which takes place in physical structures, and which forms the raw material of natural selection. And if that is so, it is evident that any attempt to prevent the play of new ideas on old institutions is striking at the very fact of progress. For if we are to encourage variation we must permit it in all directions, up as well as down, for evil as well as for good. You cannot check variation in one direction without checking it in all. You cannot prevent the appearance of a new idea that you do not want without threatening the appearance of a number of ideas that you would eagerly welcome. It is, therefore, always better to encourage the appearance of a bad idea than it is to risk the suppression of a good one. Besides, it is not always that force applied to the suppression of ideas succeeds in its object. What it often does is to cause the persecuted idea to assume a more violent form, to ensure a more abrupt break with the past than would otherwise occur, with the risk of a period of reaction before orderly progress is resumed. The only way to silence an idea is to answer it. You cannot reply to a belief with bullets, or bayonet a theory into silence. History contains many lessons, but none that is plainer than this one, and none that religious and secular tyrannies learn with greater reluctance.

The Churches admit by their practice the truth of what has been said. They have always understood that the right way to keep society in a stationary position is to prevent the introduction of new ideas. It is thought against which they have warred, the thinker against whom they have directed their deadliest weapons. The Christian Church has been tolerant towards the criminal, and has always been intolerant towards the heretic and the Freethinker. For the latter the naming *auto da fé*, for the former the moderate penance and the "go, and sin no more." The worst of its tortures were neither created for nor applied to the thief and the assassin, but were specially designed for the unbeliever. In this the Church acted with a sure instinct. The thief threatens no institution, not even that of private property. "Thou shalt not steal" is as much the law of a thieves' kitchen as it is of Mayfair. But Copernicus, Galileo, Newton, Lyell, Darwin, these are the men who convey a threat in all they write, who destroy and create with a splendour that smacks of the power with which Christians have endowed their mythical deity. No aggregation of criminals has ever threatened the security of the Church, or even disturbed its serenity. On the contrary, the worse, morally, the time, the greater the influence of Christianity. It flourishes on human weakness and social vice as the bacilli of tuberculosis do in darkness and dirt. It is when weakness gives place to strength, and darkness to light that the Church finds its power weakening. The Church could forgive the men who instituted the black slave trade, she could forgive those who were responsible for the horrors of the English factory system, but she could never forgive the writer of the *Age of Reason*. She has always known how to distinguish her friends from her foes.

Right or wrong, then, the heretic, the Freethinker, represents a figure of considerable social significance. His social value does not lie wholly in the fact of his opinions being sound or his judgment impeccable. Mere revolt or heresy can never carry that assurance with it. The important thing about the rebel is that he represents a spirit, a temper, in the absence of which society would stagnate. It is bad when people revolt without cause, but it is infinitely better that a people should revolt without cause than that they should have cause for rebellion without possessing the courage of a kick. That man should have the courage to revolt against the thing which he believes to be wrong is of infinitely greater consequence than that he should be right in condemning the thing against which he revolts. Whether the rebel is right or wrong time and consequence alone can tell, but nothing can make good the evil of a community reduced to sheep-like acquiescence in whatever may be imposed upon them. The "Their's not to reason why" attitude, however admirable in an army, is intolerable and dangerous in social life. Replying to those who shrieked about the "horrors" of the French Revolution, and who preached the virtue of patriotic obedience to established authority, Carlyle, with an eye on Ireland, sarcastically admitted that the "horrors" were very bad indeed, but he added:—

> What if history somewhere on this planet were to hear of a nation, the third soul of whom had not for thirty weeks of each year as many third-rate potatoes as would sustain him? History in that case, feels bound to consider that starvation is starvation; that starvation presupposes much; history ventures to assert that the French Sansculotte of Nine-three, who roused from a long death sleep, could rush at once to the frontiers and die fighting for an immortal hope and faith of deliverance for him and his, was but the second miserablest of men.

And that same history, looking back through the ages, is bound to confess that it is to the great rebels, from Satan onward, that the world mainly owes whatever of greatness or happiness it has achieved.

One other quality of the rebel remains to be noted. In his revolt against established authority, in his determination to wreck cherished institutions for the realization of an ideal, the rebel is not the representative of an anti-social idea or of an anti-social force. He is the true representative of the strongest of social influences. The very revolt against the social institutions that exist is in the name and for the realization of a larger and a better social order that he hopes to create. A man who is ready to sacrifice his life in the pursuit of an ideal cannot, whatever else he may be accused of, be reasonably accused of selfishness or of a want of "social consciousness." He is a vital expression of the centuries of social life which have gone before and which have made us all what we are. Were his social sense weaker he would risk less. Were he selfish he would not trouble about the conversion of his fellows. The spirit of revolt represents an important factor in the process of social development, and they who are most strenuous in their denunciation of social control, are often, even though unconsciously, the strongest evidence of its overpowering influence.

Fed as we are with the mental food prepared by our Churches and governments, to whose interests it is that the rebel and the Freethinker should be decried and denounced, we are all too apt to overlook the significance of the rebel. Yet he is invariably the one who voices what the many are afraid or unable to express. The masses suffer dumbly, and the persistence of their suffering breeds a sense of its inevitability. It is only when these dumb masses find a voice that they threaten the established order, and for this the man of ideas is essential. That is why all vested interests, religious and social, hate him so heartily. They recognize that of all the forces with which they deal an idea is the greatest and the most untamable. Once in being it is the most difficult to suppress. It is more explosive than dynamite and more shattering in its effects. Physical force may destroy a monarch, but it is only the force of an idea that can destroy a monarchy. You may destroy a church with cannon, but cannon are powerless against Church doctrines. An idea comes as near realizing the quality of indestructibility as anything we know. You may quiet anything in the world with greater ease than you may reduce a strong thinker to silence, or subdue anything with greater facility than you may subdue the idea that is born of strenuous thought. Fire may be extinguished and strife made to cease, ambition may be killed and the lust for power grow faint. The one thing that defies all and that finally conquers is the truth which strong men see and for which brave men fight.

It is thus left for the philosophy of Freethought, comprehensive here as elsewhere, to find a place for the rebel and to recognize the part he plays in the evolution of the race. For rebellion roots itself ultimately in the spirit of mental independence. And that whether a particular act of revolt may be justifiable or not. It is bred of the past, but it looks forward hopefully and fearlessly to the future, and it sees in the present the material out of which that better future may be carved. That the mass of people find in the rebel someone whom it is moved to suppress is in no wise surprising. New things are not at first always pleasant, even though they may be necessary. But the temper of mind from which rebellion springs is one that society can only suppress at its peril.

CHAPTER V
THE STRUGGLE FOR THE CHILD

If the truth of what has been said above be admitted, it follows that civilization has two fundamental aspects. On the one side there is the environment, made up—so far as civilized humanity is concerned—of the ideas, the beliefs, the customs, and the stored up knowledge of preceding generations, and on the other side we have an organism which in virtue of its education responds to the environmental stimuli in a given manner. Between the man of to-day and the man of an earlier generation the vital distinction is not that the present day one is, as an organism, better, that he has keener sight, or stronger muscles, or a brain of greater capacity, but that he has a truer perception of things, and in virtue of his enlarged knowledge is able to mould natural forces, including the impulses of his own nature, in a more desirable manner. And he can do this because, as I have already said, he inherits what previous generations have acquired, and so reaps the benefits of what they have done.

We may illustrate this in a very simple manner. One of the most striking differences between the man of to-day and the man of the past is the attitude of the two in relation to natural phenomena. To the people of not so many generations ago an eclipse was a very serious thing, fraught with the promise of disaster to mankind. The appearance of a comet was no less ominous. John Knox saw in comets an indication of the wrath of heaven, and in all countries the Churches fought with all their might against the growth of the scientific view. Away back in antiquity we meet with the same view. There is, for example, the classic case of the Greek general Nikias, who, when about to extricate his army from a dangerous position before Syracuse, was told that an eclipse of the sun indicated that the gods wished him to stay where he was for three times nine days. Nikias obeyed the oracles with the result that his army was captured. Now it is certain that no general to-day would act in that manner, and if he did it is equally certain that he would be court-martialled. Equally clear is it that comets and eclipses have ceased to infect the modern mind with terror, and are now only objects of study to the learned, and of curiosity to the unlearned. But the difference here is entirely one of knowledge. Our ancestors reacted to the appearance of a comet or an eclipse in a particular manner because their knowledge of these things was of a certain kind. It was not at all a case of feeling, or of degree of feeling, or of having a better brain, but simply a matter of reacting to an environmental influence in terms of an understanding of certain things. Had we the same conception of these things that our ancestors had we should react in the same manner. We act differently because our understanding of things is different. We may put it briefly that the kind of reaction which we make to the things around us is mainly determined by our knowledge concerning their nature.

There is one other fact that brings into prominence the importance of the kind of reaction which we make to environmental stimuli. Put briefly, we may say that an important distinction between the animal and man is that the animal passes its existence in a comparatively simple environment where the experiences are few in kind and often repeated, whereas with man the environment is very complex, the experiences are varied in character, and may be only repeated after long intervals. The consequence is that in order to get through life an animal needs a few simple instincts which automatically respond to frequently repeated experiences, while on the other hand there must be with man opportunity for the kind of response which goes under the name of intelligent action. It is this which gives us the reason, or the explanation, why of all animals the human being is born the most helpless, and why he remains helpless for a longer period than does any other. The prolonged infancy is the opportunity given to the human being to acquire the benefits of education and so to reap the full advantage of that social heritage which, as we have shown, raises him so far above the level of past generations. Or we may express the matter with the late Professor Fiske, who was the first, I think, to dwell at length upon this phenomenon, that the distinction between man and the animal world is that in the one case we have developed instincts with small capacity for education, in the other few instincts with great capacity for education.

It is often said that the Churches have failed to pay attention to education, or have not taken it seriously. That is quite wrong. It may, indeed, be said that they have never failed to attend to education, and have always taken it seriously—with disastrous results to education and to social life. Ever since the birth of the modern movement for education the Church has fought hard to maintain its control of schools, and there is every reason why this should be so. Survival in the animal world may be secured in two ways. On the one side we may have a continuance of a special sort of environment to which a given structure is properly adapted; on the other there may be a modification of the animal to meet the demands of a changing environment.

Applying this principle to the question of the Churches and education the moral is clear. The human environment changes more than that of any other animal. The mere amassing of experience and its expression in the form of new institutions or in the modification of already existing ones, is enough to effect a change in the environment of successive generations. The Christian Church, or for the matter of that, any form of religion, has before it two possible courses. Either it must maintain an environment that is as little as possible unchanged, or it must modify its body of teaching to meet the changed surroundings. As a mere matter of fact both processes go on side by side, but consciously the Churches have usually followed the course of trying to maintain an unchanged environment. This is the real significance of the attempt of the more orthodox to boycott new, or heretical literature, or lectures, or to produce a "religious atmosphere" round the child. It is an attempt to create an environment to which the child's mind will respond in a manner that is favourable to the claims and teachings of the Christian Church. The Church dare not openly and plainly throw overboard its body of doctrines to meet the needs of the modern mind; and the only thing remaining is to keep the modern mind as backward as possible in order that it may rest content with a teaching that is reminiscent of a past stage of civilization.

In this connection it is interesting to note that the struggle for the child is essentially a modern phrase. So long as the teaching of religion is in, at least, a working harmony with current knowledge and the general body of the social forces the question of religious instruction does not emerge. Life itself—social life that is—to a very considerable extent enforces religious teaching. At all events it does not violently contradict it. But as, owing to the accumulation of knowledge, views of the world and of man develop that are not in harmony with accepted religious teaching, the Churches are forced to attempt the maintenance of an environment of a special religious kind to which their teaching is adapted. Hence the growing prominence of the division of secular and sacred as things that have to do with religion and things that have not. Hence, too, the importance to the Churches of acquiring power over the child's mind before it is brought completely under the influence of an environment in which orthodox teachings can only present themselves as a gross anachronism.

Thus, one may say with absolute confidence that if in a modern environment a child was left free with regard to modern influences there is nothing that would lead to an acceptance of religion. Our ancestors grew up familiar with the idea of the miraculous and the supernatural generally because there was nothing in the existing knowledge of the world that contradicted it. But what part is there in the general education of the child in modern society that would lead to that end? So far as it is taught anything about the world it learns to regard it in terms of causation and of positive knowledge. It finds itself surrounded with machinery, and inventions, and with a thousand and one mechanical and other inventions which do not in the very remotest degree suggest the supernatural. In other words, the response of a modern child in a modern environment is of a strictly non-religious kind. Left alone it would no more become religious in the sense of believing in the religious teachings of any of the Churches than it would pass through life looking for miracles or accepting fairy tales as sober statements of historic fact. It would no more express itself in terms of religion than it would describe an eclipse in the language of our ancestors of five hundred years ago.

In self defence the Churches are thus bound to make a fight for the possession of the child. They cannot wait, because that means allowing the child to grow to maturity and then dealing with it when it is able to examine religion with some regard to its historic evolution, and with a due appreciation of the hopelessly unscientific character of the conception of the supernatural. They must, so far as they can, protect the growing child from the influence of all those environmental forces that make for the disintegration of religious beliefs. The only way in which the Churches can at all make sure of a supply of recruits is by impressing them before they are old enough to resist. As the Germany of the Kaiser is said to have militarized the nation by commencing with the schools, so the Churches hope to keep the nations religious by commencing with the children. Apart from these considerations there is no reason why religion could not wait, as other subjects wait, till the child is old enough to understand and appreciate it. But with the Churches it is literally the child or nothing.

From the point of view of citizenship the retention of religion in State schools is a manifest injustice. If ever religious instruction could be justified in any circumstances it is when the religion taught represents at least the professed beliefs of the whole of the people. But that is clearly not the case to-day. Only a section of the people can be called, even formally, Christian. Large numbers are quite opposed to Christianity, and large numbers deliberately reject all religion. How, then, can the State undertake the teaching of a religion without at the same time rousing resentment in and inflicting an injustice on a large number of its members? It cannot be done, and the crowning absurdity is that the State acknowledges the non-essential character of religion by permitting all who will to go without. In secular subjects it permits no such option. It says that all children shall receive certain tuition in certain subjects for a given period. It makes instruction in these subjects compulsory on the definite and intelligible ground that the education given is necessary to the intelligent discharge of the duties of citizenship. It does not do that in the case of religion, and it dare not do that. No government to-day would have the impudence to say that discharge of the duties of citizenship is dependent upon acceptance of the Athanasian Creed, or upon the belief in the Bible, or in an after life. And not being able to say this it is driven to the absurd position of, on the one hand saying to the people, that religion shall be taught in the State schools, and on the other, if one doesn't care to have it he may leave it alone without suffering the slightest disqualification.

Indeed, it is impossible for instruction in religion to be genuinely called education at all. If I may be allowed to repeat what I have said elsewhere on this subject, one may well ask:—

> What is it that the genuine educationalist aims at? The imparting of knowledge is, of course, essential. But, in the main, education consists in a wholesome training of mind and body, in forming habits of cleanliness, truthfulness, honesty, kindness, the development of a sense of duty and of justice. Can it be said in truth that what is called religious instruction does these things, or that instruction in them is actually inseparable from religion? Does the creation of a religious "atmosphere," the telling of stories of God or Jesus or angels or devils—I omit hell—have any influence in the direction of cultivating a sound mind in a sound body? Will anyone contend that the child has even a passing understanding of subjects over which all adults are more or less mystified? To confuse is not to instruct, to mystify is not to enlighten, the repetition of meaningless phrases can leave behind no healthy residuum in the mind. It is the development of capacity along right lines that is important, not the mere cramming of verbal formulæ. Above all, it is the function of the true teacher to make his pupil independent of him. The aim of the priest is to keep one eternally dependent upon his ministrations. The final and fatal criticism upon religious instruction is that it is not education at all.

> It may be argued that a policy of creating sentiments in favour of certain things not wholly understood by the child is followed in connection with matters other than religion. We do not wait until a child is old enough to appreciate the intellectual justification of ethics to train it in morals. And in many directions we seek to develop some tendencies and to

suppress others in accordance with an accepted standard. All this may be admitted as quite true, but it may be said in reply that these are things for which an adequate reason *can* be given, and we are sure of the child's approbation when it is old enough to appreciate what has been done. But in the case of religion the situation is altogether different. We are here forcing upon the child as true, as of the same admitted value as ordinary ethical teaching, certain religious doctrines about which adults themselves dispute with the greatest acrimony. And there is clearly a wide and vital distinction between cultivating in a child sentiments the validity of which may at any time be demonstrated, or teachings upon the truth of which practically all adults are agreed, and impressing upon it teachings which all agree may be false. We are exploiting the child in the interests of a Church. Parents are allowing themselves to be made the catspaws of priests; and it is not the least formidable of the counts against the Church's influence that it converts into active enemies of children those who should stand as their chief protectors. It is religion which makes it true that "a *child's* foes shall be those of his own household."[14]

Where the claim to force religion upon the child breaks down on such grounds as those outlined above it is quite certain that it cannot be made good upon any other ground. Historically, it is also clear that we do not find that conduct was better in those ages when the Christian religion was held most unquestioningly, but rather the reverse. The moralization of the world has, as a matter of historic fact, kept pace with the secularizing of life. This is true both as regards theory and fact. The application of scientific methods to ethical problems has taught us more of the nature of morality in the short space of three or four generations than Christian teaching did in a thousand years. And it is not with an expansion of the power and influence of religion that conduct has undergone an improvement, but with the bringing of people together in terms of secular relationships and reducing their religious beliefs to the level of speculative ideas which men may hold or reject as they think fit, so long as they do not allow them to influence their relations to one another.

On all grounds it is urgent that the child should be rescued from the clutches of the priest. It is unfair to the child to so take advantage of its trust, its innocence, and its ignorance, and to force upon it as true teachings that which we must all admit may be false, and which, in a growing number of cases, the child when it grows up either rejects absolutely or considerably modifies. It is unjust to the principle upon which the modern State rests, because it is teaching the speculative beliefs of a few with money raised from the taxation of all. The whole tendency of life in the modern State is in the direction of secularization—confining the duties and activities of the State to those actions which have their meaning and application to this life. Every argument that is valid against the State forcing religion upon the adult is valid also against the State forcing religion upon the child. And, on the other hand, it is really absurd to say that religion must be forced upon the child, but we are outraging the rights of the individual and perpetuating an intolerable wrong if we force it upon the adult. Surely the dawning and developing individuality of the child has claims on the community that are not less urgent than those of the adult.

Finally, the resolve to rescue the child from the clutches of the priest is in the interest of civilization itself. All human experience shows that a civilization that is under the control of a priesthood is doomed. From the days of ancient Egypt there is no exception to this rule. And sooner or later a people, if they are to progress, are compelled to attempt to limit the control of the priest over life. The whole of the struggle of the Reformation was fundamentally for the control of the secular power—whether life should or should not be under the control of the Church. In that contest, over a large part of Europe, the Roman Church lost. But the victory was only a very partial one. It was never complete. The old priest was driven out, but the new Presbyter remained, and he was but the old tyrant in another form. Ever since then the fight has gone on, and ever since, the Protestant minister, equally with the Catholic priest, has striven for the control of education and so to dominate the mind of the rising generation. The fight for the liberation of the child is thus a fight for the control or the directing of civilization. It is a question of whether we are to permit the priest to hold the future to ransom by permitting this control of the child, or whether we are to leave religious beliefs, as we leave other beliefs of a speculative character, to such a time as the child is old enough to understand them. It is a fight for the future of civilization.

CHAPTER VI
THE NATURE OF RELIGION

It is no mere paradox to say that religion is most interesting to those who have ceased to believe in it. The reason for this is not far to seek. Religious beliefs play so large a part in the early history of society, and are so influential in social history generally, that it is impossible to leave religion alone without forfeiting an adequate comprehension of a large part of social evolution. Human development forms a continuous record; our institutions, whatever be their nature, have their roots in the far past, and often, even when modified in form, retain their essential characteristics. No student of social history can travel far or dig deeply without finding himself in contact with religion in some form. And the mass of mankind are not yet so far removed from "primitive" humanity as to give to the study of religion an exclusively archæological interest.

Where so much is discord it is well, if it be possible, to start with a basis of agreement. And on one point, at least, there is substantial unity among critics. There is a general agreement among students of folk lore, comparative mythology, and anthropology, that religious ideas rest ultimately upon an interpretation of nature that is now generally discarded. Differing as they do on details, there is consent upon this point. It is the world of the savage that originates the religion of the savage, and upon that rests the religions of civilized man as surely as his physical structure goes back to the animal world for its beginning. And in giving birth to a religious explanation of his world the savage was only pursuing the normal path of human development. Mankind progresses through trial and error; doubtful and erroneous theories are framed before more reliable ones are established, and while truth may crown our endeavours it seldom meets us at the outset. Religious beliefs thus form man's earliest interpretation of nature. On this there is, as I have said, general agreement, and it is as well not to permit ourselves to lose sight of that in the discussion of the various theories that are put forward as to the exact nature of the stages of religious development.

In many directions the less accurate theories of things are replaced gradually and smoothly by more reliable explanations. But in religion this is not so. For many reasons, with which we are not now immediately concerned, religious beliefs are not outgrown without considerable "growing pains." And a long time after the point of view from which religious beliefs sprang has been given up, the conclusions that were based on that point of view are held to most tenaciously. And yet if one accepts the scientific story of the origins of religious ideas there seems no justification whatever for this. Religion cannot transcend its origin. Multiply nothing to infinity and the result is still nothing. Illusion can beget nothing but illusion, even though in its pursuit we may stumble on reality. And no amount of ingenuity can extract truth from falsehood.

One's surprise at the perpetuation of this particular delusion is diminished by the reflection that the period during which we have possessed anything like an exact knowledge of the character and operations of natural forces is, after all, but an infinitesimal portion of the time the race has been in existence. Three or four centuries at most cover the period during which such knowledge has been at our command, and small as this is in relation to the thousands of generations wherein superstition has reigned unchallenged, a knowledge of the laws of mental life belongs only to the latter portion. And even then the knowledge available has been till recently the possession of a class, while to-day, large masses of the population are under the domination of the crudest of superstitions. The belief that thirteen is an unlucky number, that a horse-shoe brings luck, the extent to which palmistry and astrology flourishes, the cases of witchcraft that crop up every now and again, all bear testimony to the vast mass of superstition that is still with us. The primitive mind is still alive and active, disguised though it may be by a veneer of civilization and a terribly superficial education. And when one reflects upon all the facts there is cause for astonishment that in the face of so great a dead weight of custom and tradition against a rational interpretation of the universe so much has been done and in so short a time.

In discussing religion very much turns upon the meaning of the word, and unfortunately "religion" is to-day used in so many differing and conflicting senses that without the most careful definition no one is quite sure what is meant by it. The curious disinclination of so many to avow themselves as being without a religion must also be noted. To be without a religion, or rather to be known as one who is without a religion, would seem to mark one off as apart from the rest of one's kind, and to infringe all the tribal taboos at one sweep. And very few seem to have the courage to stand alone. Mr. Augustine Birrell once said, in introducing to the House of Commons an Education Bill, that children would rather be wicked than singular. That is quite true, and it is almost as true of adults as it is of children. There is no great objection to having a religion different from that of other people, because the religions of the world are already of so varied a character that there is always companionship in difference. But to be without a religion altogether is a degree of isolation that few can stand. The consequence is that although vast numbers have given up everything that is really religious they still cling to the name. They have left the service, but they show a curious attachment to the uniform. Thus it happens that we have a religion of Socialism, a religion of Ethics, etc., and I should not be surprised to find one day a religion of Atheism—if that has not already appeared.

But all this is a mistake, and a very serious mistake. The Freethinker, or Socialist, who calls his theory of life a religion is not causing the religionist to think more highly of him, he is making his opponent think more highly of his own opinions. Imitation becomes in such a case not alone flattery, but confirmation. The Goddite does not think more highly of Freethought because it is labelled religion, he merely becomes the more convinced of the supreme value of his own faith, and still hopes for the Freethinker's return to the fold. If Freethinkers are to command the respect of the religious world they must show not only that they can get along without religion, but that they can dispense with the name also. If strength does not command respect weakness will certainly fail to secure it. And those of us who are genuinely anxious that the world should be done with false ideas and mischievous frames of mind ought to at least take care that our own speech and thought are as free from ambiguity as is possible.

There is another and deeper aspect of the matter. As I have already said, language not alone expresses thought, it also governs and directs it. Locke expressed this truth when he said, "It is impossible that men should ever truly seek, or certainly discover, the disagreement of ideas themselves whilst their thoughts flutter about, or stick only on sounds of doubtful and uncertain significance." Quite a number of theological and metaphysical conundrums would lose their significance if it were only realized that the words used are not alone of doubtful and uncertain significance, but often of no possible significance whatever. They are like counterfeit coins, which retain their value only so long as they are not tested by a proper standard. And the evil of these counterfeits is that they deceive both those who tender and those who accept them. For even though slovenliness of speech is not always the product of slovenly thought, in the long run it tends to induce it, and those who realize this need to be specially on their guard against using language which can only further confuse an already sufficiently confused public opinion, and strengthen superstitions that are already sufficiently strong without our clandestine or unintended assistance.[15]

Unfortunately, it remains a favourite policy with many writers to use and define the word religion, not in accordance with a comprehensive survey of facts, but in a way that will harmonize with existing pre-possessions. To this class belongs Matthew Arnold's famous definition of religion as "Morality touched with emotion," Professor Seeley's statement that we are entitled to call religion "any habitual and permanent admiration," or the common description of religion as consisting in devotion to an ideal. All such definitions may be set on one side as historically worthless, and as not harmonizing with the facts. Arnold's definition is in the highest degree superficial, since there exists no morality that is not touched with emotion, and on the other hand there exist phases of religion that have not any connection with morality, however slight. Professor Leuba properly rules definitions of this class out of order in the comment that, as it is "the function of words to delimitate, one defeats the purpose of language by stretching the meaning of a word until it has lost all precision and unity of meaning."[16] A definition that includes everything may as well, for all the use it is, not cover anything.

Equally faulty are those definitions that are based upon an assumed conscious effort to explain the mysteries of existence. No stranger lapse ever overtook a great thinker than occurred to Herbert Spencer when he described religion as consisting in a worship of the unknowable, and as due to the desire to explain a mystery ever pressing for interpretation. Granting the existence of an Unknowable, the sense of its presence belongs to the later stages of mental evolution, not to the earlier ones. Metaphysical and mystical theories of religion are indications of its disintegration, not of its beginnings. Primitive man began to believe in ghosts and gods for the same reasons that he believed in other things; he worshipped his gods for very concrete considerations. Even the distinction between "spiritual" and material existence is quite foreign to his mind. Such distinctions arise gradually with the progress of knowledge and its disintegrating influence on inherited beliefs. If primitive man may be credited with a philosophy, and if one may use the word in a purely convenient sense, then one may say that he is neither a dualist, nor a pluralist, but a monist. The soul or double he believes in is similar to the body he sees; the unseen forces he credits with various activities are of the same kind as those with which he is acquainted. To read our conceptions into the mind of primitive man because we use our words to explain his thoughts is a procedure that is bound to end in confusion. Man's earliest conception of things is vague and indefinite. Later, he distinguishes differences, qualitative and quantitative, his conception of things becomes more definite, and distinctions are set up that lay the foundations of science and philosophy, and which mark their separation from religion.

So far as one can see there are only two causes why people should continue to use the word religion after giving up all for which it properly stands. One is sheer conservatism. When, for instance, Thomas Paine said, "To do good is my religion," he had at least the justification of believing in a deity, but apart from this the only cause for his calling the desire to do good a religion is that there had grown up the fashion of calling one's rule of life a religion. The other cause is the ill-repute that has been attached to those who avow themselves as being without religion. Orthodoxy saw to it that they were treated as pariahs without social status, and, in many cases, legal rights. Once upon a time it was useless unless one believed in the *right* religion. Nowadays, any religion will do, or anything that one cares to call a religion. But not to have any religion at all still puts one outside the pale of respectability, and there seem to be few who can stand that. And supernatural religion—the only genuine article—being impossible with many, these may still, if they care to, save their face by professing to use the name, even if they have not the thing. Orthodoxy is very accommodating nowadays.

Leaving for a time the question of how religion actually does arise, we may turn to those writers who define religion in terms of ethics. It may be admitted that so far as the later stages of religion are concerned considerable emphasis is laid upon ethics. But we can only make religion a part of ethics by expanding the term morality so as to include everything, or by contracting it so as to exclude all the lower forms of religious belief. And any definition of religion that does not embrace all its forms is obviously inaccurate. It is not at all a question of defining the higher in terms of the lower, or the lower in terms of the higher, it is simply the need of so defining religion that our definition will cover all religions, high and low, and thus deal with their essential characteristics.

The only sense in which ethics may be said to be included in religion lies in the fact that in primitive times religion includes everything. The fear of unseen intelligences is one of the most powerful factors of which early humanity is conscious, and the necessity for conciliating them is always present. The religious ceremonies connected with eating and drinking, with lying down and rising up, with sowing and reaping, with disease, hunting, and almost every circumstance of primitive life prove this. Differentiation and discrimination arise very slowly, but one after another the various departments of life do shake off the controlling influence of religion. Ethics may, therefore, be said to originate in the shadow of religion—as do most other things—but in no sense can morality be said to owe its origin to religion. Its origin is deeper and more fundamental than religion. As a matter of practice morality is independent of religious belief and moral theory, and as a matter of theory the formulation of definite moral rules is substantially independent of religion and is an assertion of its independence. Indeed, the conflict between a growing moral sense and religion is almost as large a fact in the social sphere as the conflict between religion and science is in the intellectual one.

In all its earlier stages religion is at best non-moral. It becomes otherwise later only because of the reaction of a socialized morality on religious beliefs. Early religion is never concerned with the morality of its teaching, nor are the worshippers concerned with the morality of their gods. The sole question is what the gods desire and how best to satisfy them. We cannot even conceive man ascribing ethical qualities to his gods until he has first of all conceived them in regard to his fellow men. The savage has no *moral* reverence for his gods; they are magnified men, but not perfect ones. He worships not because he admires, but because he fears. Fear is, indeed, one of the root causes of religious belief. Professor Leuba quite admits the origin of religion is fear, but he reserves the possibility of man being occasionally placed under such favourable conditions that fear may be absent. We admit the possibility, but at present it remains a possibility only. At present all the evidence goes to prove the words of Ribot that, "The religious sentiment is composed first of all of the emotion of fear in its different degrees, from profound terror to vague uneasiness, due to faith in an unknown mysterious and impalpable power." And if that be admitted, we can scarcely find here the origin of morality.

What is here overlooked is the important fact that while religion, as such, commences in a reasoned process, morality is firmly established before mankind is even aware of its existence. A formulated religion is essentially of the nature of a theory set forth to explain or to deal with certain experiences. Morality, on the other hand, takes its rise in those feelings and instincts that are developed in animal and human societies under the pressure of natural selection. The affection of the animal for its young, of the human mother for its child, the attraction of male and female, the sympathetic feelings that bind members of the same species together, these do not depend upon theory, or even upon an intellectual perception of their value. Theory tries to account for their existence, and reason justifies their being, but they are fundamentally the product of associated life. And it is precisely because morality is the inevitable condition of associated life that it has upon religion the effect of modifying it until it is at least not too great an outrage upon the conditions of social well-being. All along we can, if we will, see how the developing moral sense forces a change in religious teaching. At one time there is nothing revolting in the Christian doctrine of election which dooms one to heaven and another to hell without the slightest regard to personal merit. At another the doctrine of eternal damnation is rejected as a matter of course. Heresy hunting and heretic burning, practised as a matter of course by one generation become highly repulsive to another. In every direction we see religious beliefs undergoing a modification under the influence of moral and social growth. It is always man who moralizes his gods; never by any chance is it the gods who moralize man.

If we are to arrive at a proper understanding of religion we can, therefore, no more assume morals to be an integral part of religion than we can assume medicine or any of the special arts, all of which may be associated with religion. It will not even do to define religion with Mr. W. H. Mallock[17] as a belief that the world "has been made and is sustained by an intelligence external to and essentially independent of it." That may pass as a definition of Theism, but Theism is only one of the phases of religion, and the idea of a creator independent of the universe is one that is quite alien to the earlier stages of religion. And to deny the name of religion to primitive beliefs is to put oneself on the level of the type of Christian who declines to call any superstition but his own religion. It is for this reason impossible to agree with Professor Leuba when he says that "the idea of a creator must take precedence of ghosts and nature beings in the making of a religion." If by precedence the order of importance, from the standpoint of later and comparatively modern forms of religion, is intended, the statement may pass. But if the precedence claimed is a time order, the reply is that, instead of the idea of a creator taking precedence of ghosts and nature beings, it is from these that the idea of a creator is evolved. It is quite true Professor Leuba holds that "belief in the existence of unseen anthropopathic beings is not religion. It is only when man enters into relation with them that religion comes into existence," but so soon as man believes in the existence of them he believes himself to be in relation with them, and a large part of his efforts is expended in making these relations of an amicable and profitable character.

A further definition of religion, first given, I think, by the late Professor Fiske, but since widely used, as a craving for "fulness of life," must be dismissed as equally faulty. For if by fulness of life is meant the desire to make it morally and intellectually richer, the answer is that this desire is plainly the product of a progressive social life, of which much that now passes for religion is the adulterated expression. Apologetically, it is an attempt so to state religion that it may evade criticism of its essential character. From one point of view this may be gratifying enough, but it is no help to an understanding of the nature of religion. And how little religion does help to a fuller life will be seen by anyone who knows the part played by organized religion in mental development and how blindly obstructive it is to new ideas in all departments of life. All these attempts to define religion in terms of ethics, of metaphysics, or as the craving after an ideal are wholly misleading. It is reading history backwards, and attributing to primitive human nature feelings and conceptions which it does not and cannot possess.

In another work[18] I have traced the origin of the belief in God to the mental state of primitive mankind, and there is no need to go over the same ground here at any length. Commencing with the indisputable fact that religion is something that is acquired, an examination of the state of mind in which primitive mankind faced, and still faces, the world, led to the conclusion that the idea of god begins in the personification of natural forces by the savage. The growth of the idea of God was there traced back to the ghost, not to the exclusion of other methods of god making, but certainly as one of its prominent causes. I must refer readers to that work who desire a more extended treatment of the god-idea.

What remains to be traced here, in order to understand the other factor that is common to religions, is the belief in a continued state of existence after death, or at least of a soul.

It has been shown to the point of demonstration by writers such as Spencer, Tylor, and Frazer, that the idea of a double is suggested to man by his experience of dreams, swoons, and allied normal and abnormal experiences. Even in the absence of evidence coming to us from the beliefs of existing tribes of savages, the fact that the ghost is always depicted as identical in appearance with the living person would be enough to suggest its dream origin. But there are other considerations that carry the proof further. The savage sees in his dreams the figures of dead men and assumes that there is a double that can get out of the body during sleep. But he also dreams of dead men, and this is also proof that the dead man still exists. Death does not, then, involve the death of the ghost, but only its removal to some other sphere of existence. Further, the likeness of sleep itself to death is so obvious and so striking that it has formed one of the most insistent features of human thought and speech. With primitive man it is far more than a figure of speech. The Melanesians put this point of view when they say, "the soul goes out of the body in some dreams, and if for some reason it does not come back the man is found dead in the morning." Death and dreaming have, therefore, this in common, they are both due to the withdrawal of the double. Hence we find a whole series of ceremonies designed to avert death or to facilitate the return of the double. The lingering of this practice is well illustrated by Sir Frederick Treves in his book, *The Other Side of the Lantern*. He there tells how he saw a Chinese mother, with the tears streaming down her face, waving at the door of the house the clothing of a recently deceased child in order to bring back the departed spirit.

Death is thus the separation of the double from the body; but if it may return, its return is not always a matter of rejoicing, for we find customs that are plainly intended to prevent the ghost recognizing the living or to find its way back to its old haunts. Thus Frazer has shown that the wearing of black is really a form of disguise. It is a method taken to disguise the living from the attentions of the dead. It is in order to avoid recognition by spirits who wish to injure them that the Tongans change their war costume at every battle. The Chinese call their best beloved children by worthless names in order to delude evil spirits. In Egypt, too, the children who were most thought of were the worst clad. In some places the corpse is never carried out through the door, but by a hole in the side of the hut, which is afterwards closed so that the ghost may not find its way back.

The ghost being conceived as at all points identical with living beings, it demands attention after death. It needs food, weapons, servants, wives. In this way there originates a whole group of burial customs, performed partly from fear of what the ghost may do if its wants are neglected. The custom of burying food and weapons with the dead thus receives a simple explanation. These things are buried with the dead man in order that their spirit may accompany his to the next world and serve the same uses there that they did here. The modern custom of scattering flowers over a grave is unquestionably a survival of this primitive belief. The killing of a wife on the husband's grave has the same origin. Her spirit goes to attend the husband in the ghost-land. In the case of a chief we have the killing of servants for the same reason. When Leonidas says, "Bury me on my shield, I will enter even Hades as a Lacedæmonian," he was exhibiting the persistence of this belief in classical times. The Chinese offer a further example by making little paper houses, filling them with paper models of the things used by the dead person, and burning them on the grave. All over the world we have the same class of customs developing from the same beliefs, and the same beliefs projected by the human mind when brought face to face with the same class of phenomena.

As the ghost is pictured as like the physical man, so the next world is more or less a replica of this. The chief distinction is that there is a greater abundance of desirable things. Hunting tribes have elysiums where there is an abundance of game. The old Norse heaven was a place where there was unlimited fighting. The gold and diamonds and rubies of the Christian heaven represent a stage of civilization where these things had acquired a special value. Social distinctions, too, are often maintained. The Caribs believe that every time they secure an enemy's head they have gained a servant in the next world. And all know the story of the French aristocrat who, when threatened with hell, replied, "God will think twice before damning a person of my quality."

Several other consequences of this service paid to the dead may be noted. The ghost being drawn to the place where the body is buried, the desire to preserve the corpse probably led to the practice of embalming. The grave becomes a place of sanctity, of pilgrimage, and of religious observance, and it has been maintained by many writers, notably by Mr. W. Simpson in his *Worship of Death*, that the service round the grave gives us the beginning of all temple worship.

But from this brief view of the beginnings of religion we are able to see how completely fallacious are all those efforts to derive religion from an attempt to achieve an ideal, from a desire to solve certain philosophical problems, or from any of the other sources that are paraded by modern apologists. The origin and nature of religion is comparatively simple to understand, once we have cleared our minds of all these fallacies and carefully examine the facts. Religion is no more than the explanation which the primitive mind gives of the experiences which it has of the world. And, therefore, the only definition that covers all the facts, and which stresses the essence of all religions, high and low, savage and civilized, is that given by Tylor, namely, the belief in supernatural beings. It is the one definition that expresses the feature common to all religions, and with that definition before us we are able to use language with a precision that is impossible so long as we attempt to read into religion something that is absent from all its earlier forms, and which is only introduced when advanced thought makes the belief in the supernatural more and more difficult to retain its hold over the human mind.

CHAPTER VII
THE UTILITY OF RELIGION

The real nature of religion being as stated, it having originated in an utterly erroneous view of things, it would seem that nothing more can be needed to justify its rejection. But the conclusion would not be correct, at least so far as the mass of believers or quasi-believers are concerned. Here the conviction still obtains that religion, no matter what its origin, still wields an enormous influence for good. The curious thing is that when one enquires "what religion is it that has exerted this beneficent influence?" the replies effectually cancel one another. Each means by religion his own religion, and each accuses the religion of the other man of all the faults with which the Freethinker accuses the whole. The avowed object of our widespread missionary activity is to save the "heathen" from the evil effects of their religion; and there is not the least doubt that if the heathen had the brute force at their command, and the impudence that we have, they would cordially reciprocate. And the efforts of the various Christian sects to convert each other is too well known to need mention. So that the only logical inference from all this is that, while all religions are, when taken singly, injurious, taken in the bulk they are sources of profound benefit.

It is not alone the common or garden order of religionist who takes up this curious position, nor is it even the better educated believer; it is not uncommon to find those who have rejected all the formal religions of the world yet seeking to discover some good that religion has done or is doing. As an illustration of this we may cite an example from Sir James Frazer, than whom no one has done more to bring home to students a knowledge of the real nature of religious beliefs. It is the more surprising to find him putting in a plea for the good done by religion, not in the present, but in the past. And such an instance, if it does nothing else, may at least serve to mitigate our ferocity towards the common type of religionist.

In an address delivered in 1909, entitled "Psyche's Task: A discourse concerning the influence of superstition on the growth of Institutions," he puts in a plea for the consideration of superstition (religion) at various stages of culture. Of its effects generally, he says:—

That it has done much harm in the world cannot be denied.
It has sacrificed countless lives, wasted untold treasures,
embroiled nations, severed friends, parted husbands and
wives, parents and children, putting swords and worse than
swords between them; it has filled gaols and madhouses with
its deluded victims; it has broken many hearts, embittered
the whole of many a life, and not content with persecuting
the living it has pursued the dead into the grave and beyond
it, gloating over the horrors which its foul imagination has
conjured up to appal and torture the survivors. It has done
all this and more.

Now this is a severe indictment, and one is a little surprised to find following that a plea on behalf of this same superstition to the effect that it has "among certain races and at certain times strengthened the respect for government, property, marriage, and human life." In support of this proposition he cites a large number of instances from various races of people, all of which prove, not what Sir James sets out to prove, but only that religious observances and beliefs have been connected with certain institutions that are in themselves admirable enough. And on this point there is not, nor can there be, any serious dispute. One can find many similar instances among ourselves to-day. But the real question at issue is a deeper one than that. It is not enough for the religionist to show that religion has often been associated with good things and has given them its sanction. The reply to this would be that if it had been otherwise religion would long since have disappeared. The essential question here is, Have the institutions named a basis in secular and social life, and would they have developed in the absence of superstition as they have developed with superstition in the field?

Now I do not see that Sir James Frazer proves either that these institutions have not a sufficient basis in secular life—he would, I imagine, admit that they have; or that they would not have developed as well in the absence of superstition as they have done with it. In fact, the whole plea that good has been done by superstition seems to be destroyed in the statements that although certain institutions "have been based partly on superstitions, it by no means follows that even among these races they have never been based on anything else," and that whenever institutions have proved themselves stable and permanent "there is a strong presumption that they rest on something more solid than superstition." So that, after all, it may well be that superstition is all the time taking credit for the working of forces that are not of its kind or nature.

Let us take the example given of the respect for human life as a crucial test. Admitting that religions have taught that to take life was a sinful act, one might well interpose with the query as to whether it was ever necessary to teach man that homicide within certain limits was a wrong thing. Pre-evolutionary sociology, which sometimes taught that man originally led an existence in which his hand was against every other man, and who, therefore, fought the battle of life strictly off his own bat, may have favoured that assumption. But that we now know is quite wrong. We know that man slowly emerged from a pre-human gregarious stage, and that in all group life there is an organic restraint on mutual slaughter. The essential condition of group life is that the nature of the individual shall be normally devoid of the desire for the indiscriminate slaughter of his fellows. And if that is true of animals, it is certainly true of man. Primitive human society does not and cannot represent a group of beings each of whom must be restrained by direct coercion from murdering the other.

In this case, therefore, we have to reckon with both biological and sociological forces, and I do not see that it needs more than this to explain all there is to explain. Human life is always associated life, and this means not alone a basis of mutual forbearance and co-operation, but a development of the sympathetic feelings which tends to increase as society develops, they being, as a matter of fact, the conditions of its growth. And whatever competition existed between tribes would still further emphasize the value of those feelings that led to effective co-operation.

The question, then, whether the anti-homicidal feeling is at all dependent upon religion is answered in the negative by the fact that it ante-dates what we may term the era of conscious social organization. That of whether religion strengthens this feeling still remains, although even that has been answered by implication. And the first thing to be noted here is that whatever may be the value of the superstitious safeguard against homicide it certainly has no value as against people outside the tribe. In fact, when a savage desires to kill an enemy he finds in superstition a fancied source of strength, and often of encouragement. Westermarck points out that "savages carefully distinguish between an act of homicide committed in their own community and one where the victim is a stranger. Whilst the former is under ordinary circumstances disapproved of, the latter is in most cases allowed and often regarded as praiseworthy." And Frazer himself points out that the belief in immortality plays no small part in encouraging war among primitive peoples,[19] while if we add the facts of the killing of children, of old men and women, and wives, together with the practice of human sacrifice, we shall see little cause to attribute the development of the feeling against homicide to religious beliefs.

In one passage in his address Sir James does show himself quite alive to the evil influence of the belief in immortality. He says:—

> It might with some show of reason be maintained that no belief has done so much to retard the economic and thereby the social progress of mankind as the belief in the immortality of the soul; for this belief has led race after race, generation after generation, to sacrifice the real wants of the living to the imaginary wants of the dead. The waste and destruction of life and property which this faith has entailed has been enormous and incalculable. But I am not here concerned with the disastrous and deplorable consequences, the unspeakable follies and crimes and miseries which have flowed in practice from the theory of a future life. My business at present is with the more cheerful side of a gloomy subject.

Every author has, of course, the fullest right to select whichever aspect of a subject he thinks deserves treatment, but all the same one may point out that it is this dwelling on the "cheerful side" of these beliefs that encourages the religionist to put forward claims on behalf of present day religion that Sir James himself would be the first to challenge. There is surely greater need to emphasize the darker side of a creed that has thousands of paid advocates presenting an imaginary bright side to the public gaze.

But what has been said of the relation of the feeling against homicide applies with no more than a variation of terms to the other instances given by Sir James Frazer. Either these institutions have a basis in utility or they have not. If they have not, then religion can claim no social credit for their preservation. If they have a basis in utility, then the reason for their preservation is to be found in social selection, although the precise local form in which an institution appears may be determined by other circumstances. And when Sir James says that the task of government has been facilitated by the superstition that the governors belonged to a superior class of beings, one may safely assume that the statement holds good only of individual governors, or of particular forms of government. It may well be that when a people are led to believe that a certain individual possesses supernatural powers, or that a particular government enjoys the favour of supernatural beings, there will be less inclination to resentment against orders than there would be otherwise. But government and governors, in other words, a general body of rules for the government of the tribe, and the admitted leadership of certain favoured individuals, would remain natural facts in the absence of superstition, and their development or suppression would remain subject to the operation of social or natural selection. So, again, with the desire for private property. The desire to retain certain things as belonging to oneself is not altogether unnoticeable among animals. A dog will fight for its bone, monkeys secrete things which they desire to retain for their own use, etc., and so far as the custom possesses advantages, we may certainly credit savages with enough common-sense to be aware of the fact. But the curious thing is that the institution of private property is not nearly so powerful among primitive peoples as it is among those more advanced. So that we are faced with this curious comment upon Sir James's thesis. Granting that the institution of private property has been strengthened by superstition we have the strange circumstance that that institution is weakest where superstition is strongest and strongest where superstition is weakest.

The truth is that Sir James Frazer seems here to have fallen into the same error as the late Walter Bagehot, and to have formed the belief that primitive man required breaking in to the "social yoke." The truth is that the great need of primitive mankind is not to be broken in but to acquire the courage and determination to break out. This error may have originated in the disinclination of the savage to obey *our* rules, or it may have been a heritage from the eighteenth century philosophy of the existence of an idyllic primitive social state. The truth is, however, that there is no one so fettered by custom as is the savage. The restrictions set by a savage society on its members would be positively intolerable to civilized beings. And if it be said that these customs required formation, the reply is that inheriting the imitability of the pre-human gregarious animal, this would form the basis on which the tyrannizing custom of primitive life is built.

There was, however, another generalization of Bagehot's that was unquestionably sound. Assuming that the first step necessary to primitive mankind was to frame a custom as the means of his being "broken in," the next step in progress was to break it, and that was a far more difficult matter. Progress was impossible until this was done, and how difficult it is to get this step taken observation of the people living in civilized countries will show. But it is in relation to this second and all important step that one can clearly trace the influence of religion. And its influence is completely the reverse of being helpful. For of all the hindrances to a change of custom there is none that act with such force as does religion. This is the case with those customs with which vested interest has no direct connection, but it operates with tenfold force where this exists. Once a custom is established in a primitive community the conditions of social life surround it with religious beliefs, and thereafter to break it means a breach in the wall of religious observances with which the savage is surrounded. And so soon as we reach the stage of the establishment of a regular priesthood, we have to reckon with the operation of a vested interest that has always been keenly alive to anything which affected its profit or prestige.

It would not be right to dismiss the discussion of a subject connected with so well-respected a name as that of Sir James Frazer and leave the reader with the impression that he is putting in a plea for current religion. He is not. He hints pretty plainly that his argument that religion has been of some use to the race applies to savage times only. We see this in such sentences as the following: "More and more, as time goes on, morality shifts its grounds from the sands of superstition to the rock of reason, from the imaginary to the real, from the supernatural to the natural.... The State has found a better reason than these old wives' fables for guarding with the flaming sword of justice the approach to the tree of life," and also in saying that, "If it can be proved that in certain races and at certain times the institutions in question have been based partly on superstition, it by no means follows that even among these races they have never been based on anything else. On the contrary ... there is a strong presumption that they rest mainly on something much more solid than superstition." In modern times no such argument as the one I have been discussing has the least claim to logical force. But that, as we all know, does not prevent its being used by full-blown religionists, and by those whose minds are only partly liberated from a great historic superstition.

It will be observed that the plea of Frazer's we have been examining argues that the function of religion in social life is of a conservative character. And so far he is correct, he is only wrong in assuming it to have been of a beneficial nature. The main function of religion in sociology is conservative, not the wise conservatism which supports an institution or a custom because of its approved value, but of the kind that sees in an established custom a reason for its continuance. Urged, in the first instance, by the belief that innumerable spirits are forever on the watch, punishing the slightest infraction of their wishes, opposition to reform or to new ideas receives definite shape and increased strength by the rise of a priesthood. Henceforth economic interest goes hand in hand with superstitious fears. Whichever way man turns he finds artificial obstacles erected. Every deviation from the prescribed path is threatened with penalties in this world and the next. The history of every race and of every science tells the same story, and the amount of time and energy that mankind has spent in fighting these ghosts of its own savage past is the measure of the degree to which religion has kept the race in a state of relative barbarism.

This function of unreasoning conservatism is not, it must be remembered, accidental. It belongs to the very nature of religion. Dependent upon the maintenance of certain primitive conceptions of the world and of man, religion dare not encourage new ideas lest it sap its own foundations. Spencer has reminded us that religion is, under the conditions of its origin, perfectly rational. That is quite true.[20] Religion meets science, when the stage of conflict arises, as an opposing interpretation of certain classes of facts. The one interpretation can only grow at the expense of the other. While religion is committed to the explanation of the world in terms of vital force, science is committed to that of non-conscious mechanism. Opposition is thus present at the outset, and it must continue to the end. The old cannot be maintained without anathematizing the new; the new cannot be established without displacing the old. The conflict is inevitable; the antagonism is irreconcilable.

It lies, therefore, in the very nature of the case that religion, as religion, can give no real help to man in the understanding of himself and the world. Whatever good religion may appear to do is properly to be attributed to the non-religious forces with which it is associated. But religion, being properly concerned with the relations between man and mythical supernatural beings, can exert no real influence for good on human affairs. Far from that being the case, it can easily be shown to have had quite an opposite effect. There is not merely the waste of energy in the direction above indicated, but in many other ways. If we confine ourselves to Christianity some conception of the nature of its influence may be formed if we think what the state of the world might have been to-day had the work of enlightenment continued from the point it had reached under the old Greek and Roman civilizations. Bacon and Galileo in their prisons, Bruno and Vanini at the stake are illustrations of the disservice that Christianity has done the cause of civilization, and the obstruction it has offered to human well-being.

Again, consider the incubus placed on human progress by the institution of a priesthood devoted to the service of supernatural beings. In the fullest and truest sense of the word a priesthood represents a parasitic growth on the social body. I am not referring to individual members of the priesthood in their capacity as private citizens, but as priests, as agents or representatives of the supernatural. And here the truth is that of all the inventions and discoveries that have helped to build up civilization not one of them is owing to the priesthood, as such. One may confidently say that if all the energies of all the priests in the whole world were concentrated on a single community, and all their prayers, formulæ, and doctrines devoted to the one end, the well-being of that community would not be advanced thereby a single iota.

Far and away, the priesthood is the greatest parasitic class the world has known. All over the world, in both savage and civilized times, we see the priesthoods of the world enthroned, we see them enjoying a subsistence wrung from toil through credulity, and from wealth through self-interest. From the savage medicine hut up to the modern cathedral we see the earth covered with useless edifices devoted to the foolish service of imaginary deities. We see the priesthood endowed with special privileges, their buildings relieved from the taxes which all citizens are compelled to pay, and even special taxes levied upon the public for their maintenance. The gods may no longer demand the sacrifice of the first born, but they still demand the sacrifice of time, energy, and money that might well be applied elsewhere. And the people in every country, out of their stupidity, continue to maintain a large body of men who, by their whole training and interest, are compelled to act as the enemies of liberty and progress.

It is useless arguing that the evils that follow religion are not produced by it, that they are casual, and will disappear with a truer understanding of what religion is. It is not true, and the man who argues in that way shows that he does not yet understand what religion is. The evils that follow religion are deeply imbedded in the nature of religion itself. All religion takes its rise in error, and vested error threatened with destruction instinctively resorts to force, fraud, and imposture, in self defence. The universality of the evils that accompany religion would alone prove that there is more than a mere accident in the association. The whole history of religion is, on the purely intellectual side, the history of a delusion. Happily this delusion is losing its hold on the human mind. Year by year its intellectual and moral worthlessness is being more generally recognized. Religion explains nothing, and it does nothing that is useful. Yet in its name millions of pounds are annually squandered and many thousands of men withdrawn from useful labour, and saddled on the rest of the community for maintenance. But here, again, economic and intellectual forces are combining for the liberation of the race from its historic incubus. Complete emancipation will not come in a day, but it will come, and its arrival will mark the close of the greatest revolution that has taken place in the history of the race.

CHAPTER VIII
FREETHOUGHT AND GOD

Why do people believe in God? If one turns to the pleas of professional theologians there is no lack of answers to the question. These answers are both numerous and elaborate, and if quantity and repetition were enough, the Freethinker would find himself hopelessly "snowed under." But on examination all these replies suffer from one defect. They should ante-date the belief, whereas they post-date it. They cannot be the cause of belief for the reason that the belief was here long before the arguments came into existence. Neither singly nor collectively do these so-called reasons correspond to the causes that have ever led a single person, at any time or at any place, to believe in a God. If they already believed, the arguments were enough to provide them with sufficient justification to go on believing. If they did not already believe, the arguments were powerless. And never, by any chance, do they describe the causes that led to the existence of the belief in God, either historically or individually. They are, in truth, no more than excuses for continuing to believe. They are never the causes of belief.

The evidence for the truth of this is at hand in the person of all who believe. Let one consider, on the one hand, the various arguments for the existence of God—the argument from causation, from design, from necessary existence, etc., then put on the other side the age at which men and women began to believe in deity, and their grasp of arguments of the kind mentioned. There is clearly no relation between the two. Leaving on one side the question of culture, it is at once apparent that long before the individual is old enough to appreciate in the slightest degree the nature of the arguments advanced he is already a believer. And if he is not a believer in his early years, he is never one when he reaches maturity, certainly not in a civilized society. And when we turn from the individual Goddite to Goddites in the mass, the assumption that they owe their belief to the philosophical arguments advanced becomes grotesque in its absurdity. To assume that the average Theist, whose philosophy is taken from the daily newspaper and the weekly sermon, derives his conviction from a series of abstruse philosophical arguments is simply ridiculous. Those who are honest to themselves will admit that they were taught the belief long before they were old enough to bring any real criticism to bear upon it. It was the product of their early education, impressed upon them by their parents, and all the "reasons" that are afterwards alleged in justification are only pleas why they should not be disturbed in their belief.

Are we in any better position if we turn from the individual to the race? Is the belief in God similar to, say, the belief in gravitation, which, discovered by a genius, and resting upon considerations which the ordinary person finds too abstruse to thoroughly understand, becomes a part of our education, and is accepted upon well established authority? Again, the facts are dead against such an assumption. It is with the race as with the individual. Science and philosophy do not precede the belief in God and provide the foundation for it, they succeed it and lead to its modification and rejection. We are, in this respect, upon very solid ground. In some form or another the belief in God, or gods, belongs to very early states of human society. Savages have it long before they have the slightest inkling of what we moderns would call a scientific conception of the world. And to assume that the savage, as we know him, began to believe in his gods because of a number of scientific reasons, such as the belief in universal causation, or any of the other profound speculations with which the modern theologian beclouds the issue, is as absurd as to attribute the belief of the Salvation Army preacher to philosophical speculations. Added to which we may note that the savage is a severely practical person. He is not at all interested in metaphysics, and his contributions to the discussions of a philosophical society would be of a very meagre character. His problem is to deal with the concrete difficulties of his everyday life, and when he is able to do this he is content.

But, on the other hand, we know that our own belief in God is descended from his belief. We know that we can trace it back without a break through generations of social culture, until we reach the savage stage of social existence. It is he who, so to speak, discovers God, he establishes it as a part of the social institutions that govern the lives of every member of the group; we find it in our immaturity established as one of those many thought-forms which determine so powerfully our intellectual development. The belief in God meets each newcomer into the social arena. It is impressed upon each in a thousand and one different ways, and it is only when the belief is challenged by an opposing system of thought that philosophical theories are elaborated in its defence.

The possibility of deriving the idea of God from scientific and philosophic thought being ruled out, what remains? The enquiry from being philosophical becomes historical. That is, instead of discussing whether there are sufficient reasons for justifying the belief in God, we are left with the question of determining the causes that led people to ever regard the belief as being solidly based upon fact. It is a question of history, or rather, one may say, of anthropology of the mental history of man. When we read of some poor old woman who has been persecuted for bewitching someone's cattle or children we no longer settle down to discuss whether witchcraft rests upon fact or not; we know it does not, and our sole concern is to discover the conditions, mental and social, which enabled so strange a belief to flourish. The examination of evidence—the legal aspect—thus gives place to the historical, and the historical finally resolves itself into the psychological. For what we are really concerned with in an examination of the idea of God is the discovery and reconstruction of those states of mind which gave the belief birth. And that search is far easier and the results far more conclusive than many imagine.

In outlining this evidence it will only be necessary to present its general features. This for two reasons. First, because a multiplicity of detail is apt to hide from the general reader many of the essential features of the truth; secondly, the fact of a difference of opinion concerning the time order of certain stages in the history of the god-idea is likely to obscure the fact of the unanimity which exists among all those qualified to express an authoritative opinion as to the nature of the conditions that have given the idea birth. The various theories of the sequence of the different phases of the religious idea should no more blind us to the fact that there exists a substantial agreement that the belief in gods has its roots in the fear and ignorance of uncivilized mankind, than the circumstance that there is going on among biologists a discussion as to the machinery of evolution should overshadow the fact that evolution itself is a demonstrated truth which no competent observer questions.

In an earlier chapter we have already indicated the essential conditions which lead to the origin of religious beliefs, and there is no need again to go over that ground. What is necessary at present is to sketch as briefly as is consistent with lucidity those frames of mind to which the belief in God owes its existence.

To realize this no very recondite instrument of research is required. We need nothing more elaborate than the method by which we are hourly in the habit of estimating each other's thoughts, and of gauging one another's motives. When I see a man laugh I assume that he is pleased; when he frowns I assume that he is angry. There is here only an application of the generally accepted maxim that when we see identical results we are warranted in assuming identical causes. In this way we can either argue from causes to effects or from effects to causes. A further statement of the same principle is that when we are dealing with biological facts we may assume that identical structures imply identical functions. The structure of a dead animal will tell us what its functions were when living as certainly as though we had the living animal in front of us. We may relate function to structure or structure to function. And in this we are using nothing more uncommon than the accepted principle of universal causation.

Now, in all thinking there are two factors. There is the animal or human brain, the organ of thought, and there is the material for thought as represented by the existing knowledge of the world. If we had an exact knowledge of the kind of brain that functioned, and the exact quantity and quality of the knowledge existing, the question as to the ideas which would result would be little more than a problem in mathematics. We could make the calculation with the same assurance that an astronomer can estimate the position of a planet a century hence. In the case of primitive mankind we do not possess anything like the exact knowledge one would wish, but we do know enough to say in rather more than a general way the kind of thinking of which our earliest ancestors were capable, and what were its products. We can get at the machinery of the primitive brain, and can estimate its actions, and that without going further than we do when we assume that primitive man was hungry and thirsty, was pleased and angry, loved and feared. And, indeed, it was because he experienced fear and pleasure and love and hate that the gods came into existence.

Of the factors which determine the kind of thinking one does, we know enough to say that there were two things certain of early mankind. We know the kind of thinking of which he was capable, and we have a general notion of the material existing for thinking. Speaking of one of these early ancestors of ours, Professor Arthur Keith says, "Piltdown man saw, heard, felt, thought and dreamt much as we do," that is, there was the same *kind* of brain at work that is at work now. And that much we could be sure of by going no farther back than the savages of to-day. But as size of brain is not everything, we are warranted in saying that the brain was of a relatively simple type, while the knowledge of the world which existed, and which gives us the material for thinking, was of a very imperfect and elementary character. There was great ignorance, and there was great fear. From these two conditions, ignorance and fear, sprang the gods. Of that there is no doubt whatever. There is scarcely a work which deals with the life of primitive peoples to-day that does not emphasize that fact. Consciously or unconsciously it cannot avoid doing so. Long ago a Latin writer hit on this truth in the well-known saying, "Fear made the gods," and Aristotle expressed the same thing in a more comprehensive form by saying that fear first set man philosophizing. The undeveloped mind troubles little about things so long as they are going smoothly and comfortably. It is when something painful happens that concern is awakened. And all the gods of primitive life bear this primal stamp of fear. That is why religion, with its persistent harking back to the primitive, with its response to the "Call of the Wild" still dwells upon the fear of the Lord as a means of arousing a due sense of piety. The gods fatten on fear as a usurer does upon the folly of his clients, and in both cases the interest demanded far outweighs the value of the services rendered. At a later stage man faces his gods in a different spirit; he loses his fear and examines them; and gods that are not feared are but poor things. They exist mainly as indisputable records of their own deterioration.

Now to primitive man, struggling along in a world of which he was so completely ignorant, the one certain thing was that the world was alive. The wind that roared, the thunder that growled, the disease that left him so mysteriously stricken, were all so many living things. The division of these living forces into good and bad followed naturally from this first conception of their nature. And whatever be the stages of that process the main lines admit of no question, nor is there any question as to the nature of the conditions that brought the gods into existence. On any scientific theory of religion the gods represent no more than the personified ignorance and fear of primitive humanity. However much anthropologists may differ as to whether the god always originates from the ghost or not, whether animism is first and the worship of the ghost secondary or not, there is agreement on that point. Whichever theory we care to embrace, the broad fact is generally admitted that the gods are the products of ignorance and fear. Man fears the gods as children and even animals fear the unknown and the dangerous.

And as the gods are born of conditions such as those outlined, as man reads his own feelings and passions and desires into nature, so we find that the early gods are frankly, obtrusively, man-like. The gods are copies of their worshippers, faithful reflections of those who fear them. This, indeed, remains true to the end. When the stage is reached that the idea of God as a physical counterpart of man becomes repulsive, it is still unable to shake off this anthropomorphic element. To the modern worshipper God must not possess a body, but he must have love, and intelligence—as though the mental qualities of man are less human than the bodily ones! They are as human as arms or legs. And every reason that will justify the rejection of the conception of the universe being ruled over by a being who is like man in his physical aspects is equally conclusive against believing the universe to be ruled over by a being who resembles man in his mental characteristics. The one belief is a survival of the other; and the one would not now be accepted had not the other been believed in beforehand.

I have deliberately refrained from discussing the various arguments put forward to justify the belief in God in order that attention should not be diverted from the main point, which is that the belief in deity owes its existence to the ignorant interpretation of natural happenings by early or uncivilized mankind. Everything here turns logically on the question of origin. If the belief in God began in the way I have outlined, the question of veracity may be dismissed. The question is one of origin only. It is not a question of man first seeing a thing but dimly and then getting a clearer vision as his knowledge becomes more thorough. It is a question of a radical misunderstanding of certain experiences, the vogue of an altogether wrong interpretation, and its displacement by an interpretation of a quite different nature. The god of the savage was in the nature of an inference drawn from the world of the savage. There was the admitted premiss and there was the obvious conclusion. But with us the premiss no longer exists. We deliberately reject it as being altogether unwarrantable. And we cannot reject the premiss while retaining the conclusion. Logically, the god of the savage goes with the world of the savage; it should have no place in the mind of the really civilized human being.

It is for this reason that I am leaving on one side all those semi-metaphysical and pseudo-philosophical arguments that are put forward to justify the belief in God. As I have already said, they are merely excuses for continuing a belief that has no real warranty in fact. No living man or woman believes in God because of any such argument. We have the belief in God with us to-day for the same reason that we have in our bodies a number of rudimentary structures. As the one is reminiscent of an earlier stage of existence so is the other. To use the expressive phrase of Winwood Reade's, we have tailed minds as well as tailed bodies. The belief in God meets each newcomer to the social sphere. It is forced upon them before they are old enough to offer effective resistance in the shape of acquired knowledge that would render its lodgement in the mind impossible. Afterwards, the dice of social power and prestige are loaded in its favour, while the mental inertia of some, and the self-interest of others, give force to the arguments which I have called mere mental subterfuges for perpetuating the belief in God.

Only one other remark need be made. In the beginning the gods exist as the apotheosis of ignorance. The reason the savage had for believing in God was that he did not know the real causes of the phenomena around him. And that remains the reason why people believe in deity to-day. Under whatever guise the belief is presented, analysis brings it ultimately to that. The whole history of the human mind, in relation to the idea of God, shows that so soon as man discovers the natural causes of any phenomenon or group of phenomena the idea of God dies out in connection therewith. God is only conceived as a cause or as an explanation so long as no other cause or explanation is forthcoming. In common speech and in ordinary thought we only bring in the name of God where uncertainty exists, never where knowledge is obtainable. We pray to God to cure a fever, but never to put on again a severed limb. We associate God with the production of a good harvest, but not with a better coal output. We use "God only knows" as the equivalent of our own ignorance, and call on God for help only where our own helplessness is manifest. The idea remains true to itself throughout. Born in ignorance and cradled in fear, it makes its appeal to the same elements to the end. And if it apes the language of philosophy, it does so only as do those who purchase a ready-made pedigree in order to hide the obscurity of their origin.

CHAPTER IX
FREETHOUGHT AND DEATH

In the early months of the European war a mortally wounded British soldier was picked up between the lines, after lying there unattended for two days. He died soon after he was brought in, and one of his last requests was that a copy of Ruskin's *Crown of Wild Olive* should be buried with him. He said the book had been with him all the time he had been in France, it had given him great comfort, and he wished it to be buried with him. Needless to say, his wish was carried out, and "somewhere in France" there lies a soldier with a copy of the *Crown of Wild Olive* clasped to his breast.

There is another story, of a commoner character, which, although different in form, is wholly similar in substance. This tells of the soldier who in his last moments asks to see a priest, accepts his ministrations with thankfulness, and dies comforted with the repetition of familiar formulæ and customary prayers. In the one case a Bible and a priest; in the other a volume of lectures by one of the masters of English prose. The difference is, at first, striking, but there is an underlying agreement, and they may be used together to illustrate a single psychological principle.

Freethinker and Christian read the record of both cases, but it is the Freethinker alone whose philosophy of life is wide enough to explain both. The Freethinker knows that the feeling of comfort and the fact of truth are two distinct things. They may coalesce, but they may be as far asunder as the poles. A delusion may be as consoling as a reality provided it be accepted as genuine. The soldier with his copy of Ruskin does not prove the truth of the teachings of the *Crown of Wild Olive*, does not prove that Ruskin said the last word or even the truest word on the subjects dealt with therein. Neither does the consolation which religion gives some people prove the truth of its teachings. The comfort which religion brings is a product of the belief in religion. The consolation that comes from reading a volume of essays is a product of the conviction of the truth of the message delivered, or a sense of the beauty of the language in which the book is written. Both cases illustrate the power of belief, and that no Freethinker was ever stupid enough to question. The finest literature in the world would bring small comfort to a man who was convinced that he stood in deadly need of a priest, and the presence of a priest would be quite useless to a man who believed that all the religions of the world were so many geographical absurdities. Comfort does not produce conviction, it follows it. The truth and the social value of convictions are quite distinct questions.

There is here a confusion of values, and for this we have to thank the influence of the Churches. Because the service of the priest is sought by some we are asked to believe that it is necessary to all. But the essential value of a thing is shown, not by the number of people who get on with it, but by the number that can get on without it. The canon of agreement and difference is applicable whether we are dealing with human nature or conducting an ordinary scientific experiment. Thus, the indispensability of meat-eating is not shown by the number of people who swear that they cannot work without it, but by noting how people fare in its absence. The drinker does not confound the abstainer; it is the other way about. In the same way there is nothing of evidential value in the protests of those who say that human nature cannot get along without religion. We have to test the statement by the cases where religion is absent. And here, it is not the Christian that confounds the Freethinker, it is the Freethinker who confounds the Christian. If the religious view of life is correct the Freethinker should be a very rare bird indeed; he should be clearly recognizable as a departure from the normal type, and, in fact, he was always so represented in religious literature until he disproved the legend by multiplying himself with confusing rapidity. Now it is the Freethinker who will not fit into the Christian scheme of things. It is puzzling to see what can be done with a man who repudiates the religious idea in theory and fact, root and branch, and yet appears to be getting on quite well in its absence. That is the awkward fact that will not fit in with the religious theory. And, other things equal, one man without religion is greater evidential value than five hundred with it. All the five hundred prove at the most is that human nature can get on with religion, but the one case proves that human nature can get on without it, and that challenges the whole religious position. And unless we take up the rather absurd position that the non-religious man is a sheer abnormality, this consideration at once reduces religion from a necessity to a luxury or a dissipation.

The bearing of this on our attitude towards such a fact as death should be obvious. During the European war death from being an ever-present fact became an obtrusive one. Day after day we received news of the death of friend or relative, and those who escaped that degree of intimacy with the unpleasant visitor, met him in the columns of the daily press. And the Christian clergy would have been untrue to their traditions and to their interests—and there is no corporate body more alert in these directions—if they had not tried to exploit the situation to the utmost. There was nothing new in the tactics employed, it was the special circumstances that gave them a little more force than was usual. The following, for example, may be accepted as typical:—

> The weight of our sorrow is immensely lightened if we can feel sure that one whom we have loved and lost has but ascended to spheres of further development, education, service, achievement, where, by and by, we shall rejoin him.

Quite a common statement, and one which by long usage has become almost immune from criticism. And yet it has about as much relation to fact as have the stories of death-bed conversions, or of people dying and shrieking for Jesus to save them. One may, indeed, apply a rough and ready test by an appeal to facts. How many cases has the reader of these lines come across in which religion has made people calmer and more resigned in the presence of death than others have been who were quite destitute of belief in religion? Of course, religious folk will repeat religious phrases, they will attend church, they will listen to the ministrations of their favourite clergyman, and they will say that their religion brings them comfort. But if one gets below the stereotyped phraseology and puts on one side also the sophisticated attitude in relation to religion, one quite fails to detect any respect in which the Freethinking parent differs from the Christian one. Does the religious parent grieve less? Does he bear the blow with greater fortitude? Is his grief of shorter duration? To anyone who will open his eyes the talk of the comfort of religion will appear to be largely cant. There are differences due to character, to temperament, to training; there is a use of traditional phrases in the one case that is absent in the other, but the incidence of a deep sorrow only serves to show how superficial are the vapourings of religion to a civilized mind, and how each one of us is thrown back upon those deeper feelings that are inseparable from a common humanity. The thought of an only son who is living with the angels brings no real solace to a parent's mind. Whatever genuine comfort is available must come from the thought of a life that has been well lived, from the sympathetic presence of friends, from the silent handclasp, which on such occasions is so often more eloquent than speech—in a word, from those healing currents that are part and parcel of the life of the race. A Freethinker can easily appreciate the readiness of a clergyman to help a mind that is suffering from a great sorrow, but it is the deliberate exploitation of human grief in the name and in the interests of religion, the manufacturing of cases of death-bed consolation and repentance, the citation of evidence to which the experience of all gives the lie, that fill one with a feeling akin to disgust.

The writer from whom I have quoted says:—

> It is, indeed, possible for people who are Agnostic or unbelieving with regard to immortality to give themselves wholly to the pursuit of truth and to the service of their fellowmen, in moral earnestness and heroic endeavour; they may endure pain and sorrow with calm resignation, and toil on in patience and perseverance. The best of the ancient Stoics did so, and many a modern Agnostic is doing so to-day.

The significance of such a statement is in no wise diminished by the accompanying qualification that Freethinkers are "missing a joy which would have been to them a well-spring of courage and strength." That is a pure assumption. They who are without religious belief are conscious of no lack of courage, and they are oppressed by no feeling of despair. On this their own statement must be taken as final. Moreover, they are speaking as, in the main, those who are fully acquainted with the Christian position, having once occupied it. They are able to measure the relative value of the two positions. The Christian has no such experience to guide him. In the crises of life the behaviour of the Freethinker is at least as calm and as courageous as that of the Christian. And it may certainly be argued that a serene resignation in the presence of death is quite as valuable as the hectic emotionalism of cultivated religious belief.

What, after all, is there in the fact of natural death that should breed irresolution, rob us of courage, or fill us with fear? Experience proves there are many things that people dread more than death, and will even seek death rather than face, or, again, there are a hundred and one things to obtain which men and women will face death without fear. And this readiness to face or seek death does not seem to be at all determined by religious belief. The millions of men who faced death during the war were not determined in their attitude by their faith in religious dogmas. If questioned they might, in the majority of cases, say that they believed in a future life, and also that they found it a source of strength, but it would need little reflection to assess the reply at its true value. And as a racial fact, the fear of death is a negative quality. The positive aspect is the will to live, and that may be seen in operation in the animal world as well as in the world of man. But this has no reference, not even the remotest, to a belief in a future life. There are no "Intimations of Immortality" here. There is simply one of the conditions of animal survival, developed in man to the point at which its further strengthening would become a threat to the welfare of the species. The desire to live is one of the conditions that secures the struggle to live, and a species of animals in which this did not exist would soon go under before a more virile type. And it is one of the peculiarities of religious reasoning that a will to live here should be taken as clear proof of a desire to live somewhere else.

The fear of death could never be a powerful factor in life; existence would be next to impossible if it were. It would rob the organism of its daring, its tenacity, and ultimately divest life itself of value. Against that danger we have an efficient guard in the operation of natural selection. In the animal world there is no fear of death, there is, in fact, no reason to assume that there exists even a consciousness of death. And with man, when reflection and knowledge give birth to that consciousness, there arises a strong other regarding instinct which effectively prevents it assuming a too positive or a too dangerous form. Fear of death is, in brief, part of the jargon of priestcraft. The priest has taught it the people because it was to his interest to do so. And the jargon retains a certain currency because it is only the minority that rise above the parrot-like capacity to repeat current phrases, or who ever make an attempt to analyse their meaning and challenge their veracity.

The positive fear of death is largely an acquired mental attitude. In its origin it is largely motived by religion. Generally speaking there is no very great fear of death among savages, and among the pagans of old Greece and Rome there was none of that abject fear of death that became so common with the establishment of Christianity. To the pagan, death was a natural fact, sad enough, but not of necessity terrible. Of the Greek sculptures representing death Professor Mahaffy says: "They are simple pictures of the grief of parting, of the recollection of pleasant days of love and friendship, of the gloom of an unknown future. But there is no exaggeration in the picture." Throughout Roman literature also there runs the conception of death as the necessary complement of life. Pliny puts this clearly in the following: "Unto all, the state of being after the last day is the same as it was before the first day of life; neither is there any more variation of it in either body or soul after death than there was before death." Among the uneducated there does appear to have been some fear of death, and one may assume that with some of even of the educated this was not altogether absent. It may also be assumed that it was to this type of mind that Christianity made its first appeal, and upon which it rested its nightmare-like conception of death and the after-life. On this matter the modern mind can well appreciate the attitude of Lucretius, who saw the great danger in front of the race and sought to guard men against it by pointing out the artificiality of the fear of death and the cleansing effect of genuine knowledge.

> So shalt thou feed on Death who feeds on men,
> And Death once dead there's no more dying then.

The policy of Christianity was the belittling of this life and an exaggeration of the life after death, with a boundless exaggeration of the terrors that awaited the unwary and the unfaithful. The state of knowledge under Christian auspices made this task easy enough. Of the mediæval period Mr. Lionel Cust, in his *History of Engraving during the Fifteenth Century*, says:—

> The keys of knowledge, as of salvation, were entirely in the hands of the Church, and the lay public, both high and low, were, generally speaking, ignorant and illiterate. One of the secrets of the great power exercised by the Church lay in its ability to represent the life of man as environed from the outset by legions of horrible and insidious demons, who beset his path throughout life at every stage up to his very last breath, and are eminently active and often triumphant when man's fortitude is undermined by sickness, suffering, and the prospect of dissolution.

F. Parkes Weber also points out that, "It was in mediæval Europe, under the auspices of the Catholic Church, that descriptions of hell began to take on their most horrible aspects."[21] So, again, we have Sir James Frazer pointing out that the fear of death is not common to the lower races, and "Among the causes which thus tend to make us cowards may be numbered the spread of luxury and the doctrines of a gloomy theology, which by proclaiming the eternal damnation and excruciating torments of the vast majority of mankind has added incalculably to the dread and horror of death."[22]

No religion has emphasized the terror of death as Christianity has done, and in the truest sense, no religion has so served to make men such cowards in its presence. Upon that fear a large part of the power of the Christian Church has been built, and men having become so obsessed with the fear of death and what lay beyond, it is not surprising that they should turn to the Church for some measure of relief. The poisoner thus did a lucrative trade by selling a doubtful remedy for his own toxic preparation. More than anything else the fear of death and hell laid the foundation of the wealth and power of the Christian Church. If it drew its authority from God, it derived its profit from the devil. The two truths that emerge from a sober and impartial study of Christian history are that the power of the Church was rooted in death and that it flourished in dishonour.

It was Christianity, and Christianity alone that made death so abiding a terror to the European mind. And society once Christianized, the uneducated could find no adequate corrective from the more educated. The baser elements which existed in the Pagan world were eagerly seized upon by the Christian writers and developed to their fullest extent. Some of the Pagan writers had speculated, in a more or less fanciful spirit, on a hell of a thousand years. Christianity stretched it to eternity. Pre-Christianity had reserved the miseries of the after-life for adults. Christian writers paved the floor of hell with infants, "scarce a span long." Plutarch and other Pagan moralists had poured discredit upon the popular notions of a future life. Christianity reaffirmed them with all the exaggerations of a diseased imagination. The Pagans held that death was as normal and as natural as life. Christianity returned to the conception current among savages and depicted death as a penal infliction. The Pagan art of living was superseded by the Christian art of dying. Human ingenuity exhausted itself in depicting the terrors of the future life, and when one remembers the powers of the Church, and the murderous manner in which it exercised them, there is small wonder that under the auspices of the Church the fear of death gained a strength it had never before attained.

Small wonder, then, that we still have with us the talk of the comfort that Christianity brings in the face of death. Where the belief in the Christian after-life really exists, the retention of a conviction of the saving power of Christianity is a condition of sanity. Where the belief does not really exist, we are fronted with nothing but a parrot-like repetition of familiar phrases. The Christian talk of comfort is thus, on either count, no more than a product of Christian education. Christianity does not make men brave in the presence of death, that is no more than a popular superstition. What it does is to cover a natural fact with supernatural terrors, and then exploit a frame of mind that it has created. The comfort is only necessary so long as the special belief is present. Remove that belief and death takes its place as one of the inevitable facts of existence, surrounded with all the sadness of a last farewell, but rid of all the terror that has been created by religion.

Our dying soldier, asking for a copy of the *Crown of Wild Olive* to be buried with him, and the other who calls for priestly ministrations, represent, ultimately, two different educational results. The one is a product of an educational process applied during the darkest periods of European history, and perpetuated by a training that has been mainly directed by the self-interest of a class. The other represents an educational product which stands as the triumph of the pressure of life over artificial dogmas. The Freethinker, because he is a Freethinker, needs none of those artificial stimulants for which the Christian craves. And he pays him the compliment—in spite of his protests—of believing that without his religion the Christian would display as much manliness in the face of death as he does himself. He believes there is plenty of healthy human nature in the average Christian, and the

Freethinker merely begs him to give it a chance of finding expression. In this matter, it must be observed, the Freethinker makes no claim to superiority over the Christian; it is the Christian who forces that claim upon him. The Freethinker does not assume that the difference between himself and the Christian is nearly so great as the latter would have him believe. He believes that what is dispensable by the one, without loss, is dispensable by the other. If Freethinkers can devote themselves to "the pursuit of truth and the service of their fellow men," if they can "endure pain and sorrow with calm resignation," if they live with honour and face death without fear, I see no reason why the Christian should not be able to reach the same level of development. It is paying the Freethinker a "violent compliment," to use an expression of John Wesley's, to place him upon a level of excellence that is apparently so far above that of the average Christian. As a Freethinker, I decline to accept it. I believe that what the Freethinker is, the Christian may well become. He, too, may learn to do his duty without the fear of hell or the hope of heaven. All that is required is that he shall give his healthier instincts an opportunity for expression.

CHAPTER X
THIS WORLD AND THE NEXT

In the preceding chapter I have only discussed the fact of death in relation to a certain attitude of mind. The question of the survival of the human personality after death is a distinct question and calls for separate treatment. Nor is the present work one in which that topic can be treated at adequate length. The most that can now be attempted is a bird's eye view of a large field of controversy, although it may be possible in the course of that survey to say something on the more important aspects of the subject.

And first we may notice the curious assumption that the man who argues for immortality is taking a lofty view of human nature, while he who argues against it is taking a low one. In sober truth it is the other way about. Consider the position. It is tacitly admitted that if human motive, considered with reference to this world alone, is adequate as an incentive to action, and the consequences of actions, again considered with reference to this world, are an adequate reward for endeavour, then it is agreed that the main argument for the belief in immortality breaks down. To support or to establish the argument it is necessary to show that life divorced from the conception of a future life can never reach the highest possible level. Natural human society is powerless in itself to realize its highest possibilities. It remains barren of what it might be, a thing that may frame ideals, but can never realize them.

Now that is quite an intelligible, and, therefore, an arguable proposition. But whether true or not, there should be no question that it involves a lower view of human nature than the one taken by the Freethinker. He does at least pay human nature the compliment of believing it capable, not alone of framing high ideals, but also of realizing them. He says that by itself it is capable of realizing all that may be legitimately demanded from it. He does not believe that supernatural hopes or fears are necessary to induce man to live cleanly, or die serenely, or to carry out properly his duties to his fellows. The religionist denies this, and asserts that some form of supernaturalism is essential to the moral health of men and women. If the Freethinker is wrong, it is plain that his fault consists in taking a too optimistic view of human nature. His mistake consists in taking not a low view of human nature, but a lofty one. Substantially, the difference between the two positions is the difference between the man who is honest from a conviction of the value of honesty, and the one who refrains from stealing because he feels certain of detection, or because he is afraid of losing something that he might otherwise gain. Thus, we are told by one writer that:—

> If human life is but a by-product of the unconscious play of physical force, like a candle flame soon to be blown out or burnt out, what a paltry thing it is!

But the questions of where human life came from, or where it will end, are quite apart from the question of the value and capabilities of human life now. That there are immense possibilities in this life none but a fool will deny. The world is full of strange and curious things, and its pleasures undoubtedly outweigh its pains in the experience of normal man or woman. But the relations between ourselves and others remain completely unaffected by the termination of existence at the grave, or its continuation beyond. It is quite a defensible proposition that life is not worth living. So is the reverse of the proposition. But it is nonsense to say that life is a "paltry thing" merely because it ends at the grave. It is unrestricted egotism manifesting itself in the form of religious conviction. One might as well argue that a sunset ceases to be beautiful because it does not continue all night.

If I cannot live for ever, then is the universe a failure! That is really all that the religious argument amounts to. And so to state it, to reduce it to plain terms, and divest it of its disguising verbiage, almost removes the need for further refutation. But it is seldom stated in so plain and so unequivocal a manner. It is accompanied with much talk of growth, of an evolutionary purpose, of ruined lives made good, thus:

> Seeing that man is the goal towards which everything has tended from the beginning, seeing that the same eternal and infinite Energy has laboured through the ages at the production of man, and man is the heir of the ages, nothing conceivable seems too great or glorious to believe concerning his destiny.... If there is no limit to human growth in knowledge and wisdom, in love and constructive power, in beauty and joy, we are invested with a magnificent worth and dignity.

So fallacy and folly run on. What, for example, does anyone mean by man as the goal towards which everything has tended since the beginning? Whatever truth there is in the statement applies to all things without exception. It is as true of the microbe as it is of man. If the "infinite and eternal Energy" laboured to produce man, it laboured also to produce the microbe which destroys him. The one is here as well as the other; and one can conceive a religious microbe thanking an almighty one for having created it, and declaring that unless it is to live for ever in some microbic heaven, with a proper supply of human beings for its nourishment, the whole scheme of creation is a failure. It is quite a question of the point of view. As a matter of fact there are no "ends" in nature. There are only results, and each result becomes a factor in some further result. It is human folly and ignorance which makes an end of a consequence.

After all, what reason is there for anyone assuming that the survival of man beyond the grave is even probably true? We do not know man as a "soul" first and a body afterwards. Neither do we know him as a detached "mind" which afterwards takes possession of a body. Our knowledge of man commences with him, as does our knowledge of any animal, as a body possessing certain definite functions of which we call one group mental. And the two things are so indissolubly linked that we cannot even think of them as separate. If anyone doubts this let him try and picture to himself what a man is like in the absence of a body. He will find the thing simply inconceivable. In the absence of the material organism, to which the mind unquestionably stands in the relation of function to organ, what remains is a mere blank. To the informed mind, that is. To the intelligence of the savage, who is led, owing to his erroneous conception of things, to think of something inside the body which leaves it during sleep, wanders about, and then returns on awakening, and who because of this affiliates sleep to death, the case may be different. But to a modern mind, one which is acquainted with something of what science has to say on the subject, the conception of a mind existing apart from organization is simply unthinkable. All our knowledge is against it. The development of mind side by side with the development of the brain and the nervous system is one of the commonplaces of scientific knowledge. The treatment of states of mind as functions of the brain and the nervous system is a common-place of medical practice. And the fact that diet, temperature, health and disease, accidents and old age, all have their effects on mental manifestations is matter of everyday observation. The whole range of positive science may safely be challenged to produce a single indisputable fact in favour of the assumption that there exists anything about man independent of the material organism.

All that can be urged in favour of such a belief is that there are still many obscure facts which we are not altogether able to explain on a purely mechanistic theory. But that is a confession of ignorance, not an affirmation of knowledge. At any rate, there does not exist a single fact against the functional theory of mind. All we *know* is decidedly in its favour, and a theory must be tested by what we know and by what it explains, not by what we do not know or by what it cannot explain. And there is here the additional truth that the only ground upon which the theory can be opposed is upon certain metaphysical assumptions which are made in order to bolster up an already existing belief. If the belief in survival had not been already in existence these assumptions would never have been made. They are not suggested by the facts, they are invented to support an already established theory, which can no longer appeal to the circumstances which gave it birth.

And about those circumstance there is no longer the slightest reason for justifiable doubt. We can trace the belief in survival after death until we see it commencing in the savage belief in a double that takes its origin in the phenomena of dreaming and unusual mental states. It is from that starting point that the belief in survival takes its place as an invariable element in the religions of the world. And as we trace the evolution of knowledge we see every fact upon which was built the belief in a double that survived death gradually losing its hold on the human intelligence, owing to the fact that the experiences that gave it birth are interpreted in a manner which allows no room for the religious theory. The fatal fact about the belief in survival is its history. That history shows us how it began, as surely as the course of its evolution indicates the way in which it will end.

So, as with the idea of God, what we have left in modern times are not the reasons why such a belief is held, but only excuses why those who hold it should not be disturbed. That and a number of arguments which only present an air of plausibility because they succeed in jumbling together things that have no connection with each other. As an example of this we may take the favourite modern plea that a future life is required to permit the growth and development of the individual. We find this expressed in the quotation above given in the sentence "if there is no limit to human growth, etc.," the inference being that unless there is a future life there is a very sharp limit set to human growth, and one that makes this life a mockery. This plea is presented in so many forms that it is worth while analysing it a little, if only to bring out more clearly the distinction between the religious and the Freethought view of life.

What now is meant by there being no limit to human growth? If by it is meant individual growth, the reply is that there is actually a very sharp limit set to growth, much sharper than the average person seems to be aware of. It is quite clear that the individual is not capable of unlimited growth in this world. There are degrees of capacity in different individuals which will determine what amount of development each is capable of. Capacity is not an acquired thing, it is an endowment, and the child born with the brain capacity of a fool will remain a fool to the end, however much his folly may be disguised or lost amid the folly of others. And with each one, whether he be fool or genius, acquisitions are made more easily and more rapidly in youth, the power of mental adaptation is much greater in early than in later life, while in old age the capacities of adaptation and acquisition become negligible quantities. And provided one lives long enough, the last stage sees, not a promise of further progress if life were continued, but a process of degradation. The old saying that one can't put a quart into a pint pot is strictly applicable here. Growth assumes acquisition; acquisition is determined by capacity, and this while an indefinite quantity (indefinite here is strictly referable to our ignorance, not to the actual fact) is certainly not an unlimited one. Life, then, so far as the individual is concerned, does not point to unlimited growth. It indicates, so far as it indicates anything at all, that there is a limit to growth as to all other things.

Well, but suppose we say that man is capable of indefinite growth, what do we mean? Let us also bear in mind at this point that we are strictly concerned with the individual. For if man survives death he must do it as an individual. To merely survive as a part of the chemical and other elements of the world, or, to follow some mystical theologians, as an indistinguishable part of a "world-soul," is not what people mean when they talk of living beyond the grave. Here, again, it will be found that we have confused two quite distinct things, even though the one thing borrows its meaning from the other.

When we compare the individual, as such, with the individual of three or four thousand years ago, can we say with truth that the man of to-day is actually superior to the man of the earlier date? To test the question let us put it in this way. Does the man of to-day do anything or think anything that is beyond the capacity of an ancient Egyptian or an ancient Greek, if it were possible to suddenly revive one and to enable him to pass through the same education that each one of us passes through? I do not think that anyone will answer that question in the affirmative. Reverse the process. Suppose that a modern man, with exactly the same capacity that he now has had lived in the days of the ancient Egyptians or the ancient Greeks, can we say that his capacity is so much greater than theirs, that he would have done better than they did? I do not think that anyone will answer that question in the affirmative either. Is the soldier of to-day a better soldier, or the sailor a better sailor than those who lived three thousand years ago? Once more the answer will not be in the affirmative. And yet there are certain things that are obvious. It is plain that we all know more than did the people of long ago, we can do more, we understand the past better, and we can see farther into the future. A schoolboy to-day carries in his head what would have been a philosopher's outfit once upon a time. Our soldiers and sailors utilize, single-handed, forces greater than a whole army or navy wielded in the far-off days of the Ptolemies. We call ourselves greater, we think ourselves greater, and in a sense we are greater than the people of old. What, then, is the explanation of the apparent paradox?

The explanation lies in the simple fact that progress is not a phenomenon of individual life at all. It is a phenomenon of social existence. If each generation had to commence at the exact point at which its predecessors started it would get no farther than they got. It would be an eternal round, with each generation starting from and reaching the same point, and progress would be an inconceivable thing. But that we know is not the case. Instead of each generation starting from precisely the same point, one inherits at least something of the labours and discoveries of its predecessors. A thing discovered by the individual is discovered for the race. A thought struck out by the individual is a thought for the race. By language, by tradition, and by institutions the advances of each generation are conserved, handed on, and made part of our racial possessions. The strength, the knowledge, of the modern is thus due not to any innate superiority over the ancient, but because one is modern and the other ancient. If we could have surrounded the ancient Assyrians with all the inventions, and given them all the knowledge that we possess, they would have used that knowledge and those inventions as wisely, or as unwisely as we use them. Progress is thus not a fact of individual but of racial life. The individual inherits more than he creates, and it is in virtue of this racial inheritance that he is what he is.

It is a mere trick of the imagination that converts this fact of social growth into an essential characteristic of individual life. We speak of "man" without clearly distinguishing between man as a biological unit and man as a member of a social group developing in correspondence with a true social medium. But if that is so, it follows that this capacity for growth is, so to speak, a function of the social medium. It is conditioned by it, it has relevance only in relation to it. Our feelings, our sentiments, even our desires, have reference to this life, and in a far deeper sense than is usually imagined. And removed from its relation to this life human nature would be without meaning or value.

There is nothing in any of the functions of man, in any of his capacities, or in any of his properly understood desires that has the slightest reference to any life but this. It is unthinkable that there should be. An organ or an organism develops in relation to a special medium, not in relation to one that— even though it exists—is not also in relation with it. This is quite an obvious truth in regard to structures, but it is not always so clearly recognized, or so carefully borne in mind, that it is equally true of every feeling and desire. For these are developed in relation to their special medium, in this case, the existence of fellow beings with their actions and reactions on each other. And man is not only a member of a social group, that much is an obvious fact; but he is a product of the group in the sense that all his characteristic human qualities have resulted from the interactions of group life. Take man out of relation to that fact, and he is an enigma, presenting fit opportunities for the wild theorizing of religious philosophers. Take him in connection with it, and his whole nature becomes susceptible of understanding in relation to the only existence he knows and desires.

The twin facts of growth and progress, upon which so much of the argument for a future life turns nowadays, have not the slightest possible reference to a life beyond the grave. They are fundamentally not even personal, but social. It is the race that grows, not the individual, he becomes more powerful precisely because the products of racial acquisition are inherited by him. Remove, if only in thought, the individual from all association with his fellows, strip him of all that he inherits from association with them, and he loses all the qualities we indicate when we speak of him as a civilized being. Remove him, in fact, from that association, as when a man is marooned on a desert island, and the more civilized qualities of his character begin to weaken and in time disappear. Man, as an individual, becomes more powerful with the passing of each generation, precisely because he is thus dependent upon the life of the race. The secret of his weakness is at the same time the source of his strength. We are what we are because of the generations of men and women who lived and toiled and died before we were born. We inherit the fruits of their labours, as those who come after us will inherit the fruits of our struggles and conquests. It is thus in the life of the race that man achieves immortality. None other is possible, or conceivable. And to those whose minds are not distorted by religious teaching, and who have taken the trouble to analyse and understand their own mental states, it may be said that none other is even desirable.

CHAPTER XI
EVOLUTION

Language, we have said above, is one of the prime conditions of human greatness and progress. It is the principal means by which man conserves his victories over the forces of his environment, and transmits them to his descendants. But it is, nevertheless, not without its dangers, and may exert an influence fatal to exact thought. There is a sense in which language necessarily lags behind thought. For words are coined to express the ideas of those who fashion them; and as the knowledge of the next generation alters, and some modification of existing conceptions is found necessary, there is nothing but the existing array of words in which to express them. The consequence is that there are nearly always subtle shades of meaning in the words used differing from the exact meaning which the new thought is trying to express. Thought drives us to seek new or improved verbal tools, but until we get them we must go on using the old ones, with all their old implications. And by the time the new words arrive thought has made a still further advance, and the general position remains. It is an eternal chase in which the pursued is always being captured, but is never caught.

Another way in which language holds a danger is that with many words, especially when they assume the character of a formula, they tend to usurp the place of thinking. The old lady who found so much consolation in the "blessed" word Mesopotamia, is not alone in using that method of consolation. It does not meet us only in connection with religion, it is encountered over the whole field of sociology, and even of science. A conception in science or sociology is established after a hard fight. It is accepted generally, and thereafter takes its place as one of the many established truths. And then the danger shows itself. It is repeated as though it had some magical virtue in itself; it means nothing to very many of those who use it, they simply hand over their mental difficulties to its care, much as the penitent in the confessional hands over his moral troubles to the priest, and there the matter ends. But in such cases the words used do not express thought, they simply blind people to its absence. And not only that, but in the name of these sacred words, any number of foolish inferences are drawn and receive general assent.

A striking illustration of this is to be found in such a word as "Evolution." One may say of it that while it began as a formula, it continues as a fiat. Some invoke it with all the expectancy of a mediæval magician commanding the attendance of his favourite spirits. Others approach it with a hushed reverence that is reminiscent of a Catholic devotee before his favourite shrine. In a little more than half a century it has acquired the characteristics of the Kismet of the Mohammedan, the Beelzebub of the pious Christian, and the power of a phrase that gives inspiration to a born soldier. It is used as often to dispel doubt as it is to awaken curiosity. It may express comprehension or merely indicate vacuity. Decisions are pronounced in its name with all the solemnity of a "Thus saith the Lord." We are not sure that even to talk about evolution in this way may not be considered wrong. For there are crowds of folk who cannot distinguish profundity from solemnity, and who mistake a long face for the sure indication of a well-stored brain. The truth here is that what a man understands thoroughly he can deal with easily; and that he laughs at a difficulty is not necessarily a sign that he fails to appreciate it, he may laugh because he has taken its measure. And why people do not laugh at such a thing as religion is partly because they have not taken its measure, partly from a perception that religion cannot stand it. Everywhere the priest maintains his hold as a consequence of the narcotizing influence of ill-understood phrases, and in this he is matched by the pseudo-philosopher whose pompous use of imperfectly appreciated formulæ disguises from the crowd the mistiness of his understanding.

A glance over the various uses to which the word "Evolution" is put will well illustrate the truth of what has been said. These make one wonder what, in the opinion of some people, evolution stands for. One of these uses of evolution is to give it a certain moral implication to which it has not the slightest claim. A certain school of Non-Theists are, in this matter, if not the greatest offenders, certainly those with the least excuse for committing the blunder. By these evolution is identified with progress, or advancement, or a gradual "levelling up" of society, and is even acclaimed as presenting a more "moral" view of the Universe than is the Theistic conception. Now, primarily, this ascription of what one may call a moral element to evolution is no more than a carrying over into science of a frame of mind that properly belongs to Theism. Quite naturally the Theist was driven to try and find some moral purpose in the Universe, and to prove that its working did not grate on our moral sense. That was quite understandable, and even legitimate. The world, from the point of view of the Goddite, was God's world, he made it; and we are ultimately compelled to judge the character of God from his workmanship. An attack on the moral character of the world is, therefore, an attack on the character of its maker. And the Theist proceeded to find a moral justification for all that God had done.

So far all is clear. But now comes a certain kind of Non-Theist. And he, always rejecting a formal Theism and substituting evolution, proceeds to claim for his formula all that the Theist claimed for his. He also strives to show that the idea of cosmic evolution involves conceptions of nobility, justice, morality, etc. There is no wonder that some Christians round on him, and tell him that he still believes in a god. Substantially he does. That is, he carries over into his new camp the same anthropomorphic conception of the workings of nature, and uses the same pseudo-scientific reasoning that is characteristic of the Theist. He has formally given up God, but he goes about uncomfortably burdened with his ghost.

Now, evolution is not a fiat, but a formula. It has nothing whatever to do with progress, as such, nor with morality, as such, nor with a levelling up, nor a levelling down. It is really no more than a special application of the principle of causation, and whether the working out of that principle has a good effect or a bad one, a moralizing, or a demoralizing, a progressive, or a retrogressive consequence is not "given" in the principle itself. Fundamentally, all cosmic phenomena present us with two aspects— difference and change—and that is so because it is the fundamental condition of our knowing anything at all. But the law of evolution is no more, is nothing more serious or more profound than an attempt to express those movements of change and difference in a more or less precise formula. It aims at doing for phenomena in general exactly what a particular scientific law aims at doing for some special department. But it has no more a moral implication, or a progressive implication than has the law of gravitation or of chemical affinity. The sum of those changes that are expressed in the law of evolution may result in one or the other; it has resulted in one or the other. At one time we call its consequences moral or progressive, at another time we call them immoral or retrogressive, but these are some of the distinctions which the human mind creates for its own convenience, they have no validity in any other sense. And when we mistake these quite legitimate distinctions, made for our own convenience, and argue as though they had an actual independent existence, we are reproducing exactly the same mental confusion that keeps Theism alive.

The two aspects that difference and change resolve themselves into when expressed in an evolutionary formula are, in the inorganic world, equilibrium, and, in the organic world, adaptation. Of course, equilibrium also applies to the organic world, I merely put it this way for the purpose of clarity. Now, if we confine our attention to the world of animal forms, what we have expressed, primarily, is the fact of adaptation. If an animal is to live it must be adapted to its surroundings to at least the extent of being able to overcome or to neutralize the forces that threaten its existence. That is quite a common-place, since all it says is that to live an animal must be fit to live, but all great truths are common-places—when one sees them. Still, if there were only adaptations to consider, and if the environment to which adaptation is to be secured, remained constant, all we should have would be the deaths of those not able to live, with the survival of those more fortunately endowed. There would be nothing that we could call, even to please ourselves, either progress or its reverse. Movement up or down (both human landmarks) occurs because the environment itself undergoes a change. Either the material conditions change, or the pressure of numbers initiates a contest for survival, although more commonly one may imagine both causes in operation at the same time. But the consequence is the introduction of a new quality into the struggle for existence. It becomes a question of a greater endowment of the qualities that spell survival. And that paves the way to progress—or the reverse. But one must bear in mind that, whether the movement be in one direction or the other, it is still the same process that is at work. Evolution levels neither "up" nor "down." Up and down is as relative in biology as it is in astronomy. In nature there is neither better nor worse, neither high nor low, neither good nor bad, there are only differences, and if that had been properly appreciated by all, very few of the apologies for Theism would ever have seen the light.

There is not the slightest warranty for speaking of evolution as being a "progressive force," it is, indeed, not a force at all, but only a descriptive term on all fours with any other descriptive term as expressed in a natural law. It neither, of necessity, levels up nor levels down. In the animal world it illustrates adaptation only, but whether that adaptation involves what we choose to call progression or retrogression is a matter of indifference. On the one hand we have aquatic life giving rise to mammalian life, and on the other hand, we have mammalian life reverting to an aquatic form of existence. In one place we have a "lower" form of life giving place to a "higher" form. In another place we can see the reverse process taking place. And the "lower" forms are often more persistent than the "higher" ones, while, as the course of epidemical and other diseases shows certain lowly forms of life may make the existence of the higher forms impossible. The Theistic attempt to disprove the mechanistic conception of nature by insisting that evolution is a law of progress, that it implies an end, and indicates a goal, is wholly fallacious. From a scientific point of view it is meaningless chatter. Science knows nothing of a plan, or an end in nature, or even progress. All these are conceptions which we humans create for our own convenience. They are so many standards of measurement, of exactly the same nature as our agreement that a certain length of space shall be called a yard, or a certain quantity of liquid shall be called a pint. To think otherwise is pure anthropomorphism. It is the ghost of God imported into science.

So far, then, it is clear that the universal fact in nature is change. The most general aspect of nature which meets us is that expressed in the law of evolution. And proceeding from the more general to the less general, in the world of living beings this change meets us in the form of adaptation to environment. But what constitutes adaptation must be determined by the nature of the environment. That will determine what qualities are of value in the struggle for existence, which is not necessarily a struggle against other animals, but may be no more than the animal's own endeavours to persist in being. It is, however, in relation to the environment that we must measure the value of qualities. Whatever be the nature of the environment that principle remains true. Ideally, one quality may be more desirable than another, but if it does not secure a greater degree of adaptation to the environment it brings no advantage to its possessor. It may even bring a positive disadvantage. In a thieves' kitchen the honest man is handicapped. In a circle of upright men the dishonest man is at a discount. In the existing political world a perfectly truthful man would be a parliamentary failure. In the pulpit a preacher who knew the truth about Christianity and preached it would soon be out of the Church. Adaptation is not, as such, a question of moral goodness or badness, it is simply adaptation.

A precautionary word needs be said on the matter of environment. If we conceive the environment as made up only of the material surroundings we shall not be long before we find ourselves falling into gross error. For that conception of environment will only hold of the very lowest organisms. A little higher, and the nature of the organism begins to have a modifying effect on the material environment, and when we come to animals living in groups the environment of the individual animal becomes partly the habits and instincts of the other animals with which it lives. Finally, when we reach man this transformation of the nature of the environment becomes greatest. Here it is not merely the existence of other members of the same species, with all their developed feelings and ideas to which each must become adapted to live, but in virtue of what we have described above as the social medium, certain "thought forms" such as institutions, conceptions of right and wrong, ideals of duty, loyalty, the relation of one human group to other human groups, not merely those that are now living, but also those that are dead, are all part of the environment to which adjustment must be made. And in the higher stages of social life these aspects of the environment become of even greater consequence than the facts of a climatic, geographic, or geologic nature. In other words, the environment which exerts a predominating influence on civilized mankind is an environment that has been very largely created by social life and growth.

If we keep these two considerations firmly in mind we shall be well guarded against a whole host of fallacies and false analogies that are placed before us as though they were unquestioned and unquestionable truths. There is, for instance, the misreading of evolution which asserts that inasmuch as what is called moral progress takes place, therefore evolution involves a moral purpose. We find this view put forward not only by avowed Theists, but by those who, while formally disavowing Theism, appear to have imported into ethics all the false sentiment and fallacious reasoning that formerly did duty in bolstering up the idea of God. Evolution, as such, is no more concerned with an ideal morality than it is concerned with the development of an ideal apple dumpling. In the universal process morality is no more than a special illustration of the principle of adaptation. The morality of man is a summary of the relations between human beings that must be maintained if the two-fold end of racial preservation and individual development are to be secured. Fundamentally morality is the formulation in either theory or practice of rules or actions that make group-life possible. And the man who sees in the existence or growth of morality proof of a "plan" or an "end" is on all fours with the mentality of the curate who saw the hand of Providence in the fact that death came at the end of life instead of in the middle of it. What we are dealing with here is the fact of adaptation, although in the case of the human group the traditions and customs and ideals of the group form a very important part of the environment to which adaptation must be made and have, therefore, a distinct survival value. The moral mystery-monger is only a shade less objectionable than the religious mystery-monger, of whom he is the ethical equivalent.

A right conception of the nature of environment and the meaning of evolution will also protect us against a fallacy that is met with in connection with social growth. Human nature, we are often told, is always the same. To secure a desired reform, we are assured, you must first of all change human nature, and the assumption is that as human nature cannot be changed the proposed reform is quite impossible.

Now there is a sense in which human nature is the same, generation after generation. But there is another sense in which human nature is undergoing constant alteration, and, indeed, it is one of the outstanding features of social life that it should be so. So far as can be seen there exists no difference between the fundamental capacities possessed by man during at least the historic period. There are differences in people between the relative strengths of the various capacities, but that is all. An ancient Assyrian possessed all the capacities of a modern Englishman, and in the main one would feel inclined to say the same of them in their quantitative aspect as well as in their qualitative one. For when one looks at the matter closely it is seen that the main difference between the ancient and the modern man is in expression. Civilization does not so much change the man so much as it gives a new direction to the existing qualities. Whether particular qualities are expressed in an ideally good direction or the reverse depends upon the environment to which they react.

To take an example. The fundamental evil of war in a modern state is that it expends energy in a harmful direction. But war itself, the expression of the war-like character, is the outcome of pugnacity and the love of adventure without which human nature would be decidedly the poorer, and would be comparatively ineffective. It is fundamentally an expression of these qualities that lead to the quite healthy taste for exploration, discovery, and in intellectual pursuits to that contest of ideas which lies at the root of most of our progress. And what war means in the modern State is that the love of competition and adventure, the pugnacity which leads a man to fight in defence of a right or to redress a wrong, and without which human nature would be a poor thing, are expended in the way of sheer destruction instead of through channels of adventure and healthy intellectual contest. Sympathies are narrowed instead of widened, and hatred of the stranger and the outsider, of which a growing number of people in a civilized country are becoming ashamed, assumes the rank of a virtue. In other words, a state of war creates an environment—fortunately for only a brief period—which gives a survival value to such expressions of human capacity as indicate a reversion to a lower state of culture.

We may put the matter thus. While conduct is a function of the organism, and while the *kind* of reaction is determined by structure, the *form* taken by the reaction is a matter of response to environmental influences. It is this fact which explains why the capacities of man remain fairly constant, while there is a continuous redirecting of these capacities into new channels suitable to a developing social life.

We are only outlining here a view of evolution that would require a volume to discuss and illustrate adequately, but enough has been said to indicate the enormous importance of the educative power of the environment. We cannot alter the capacities of the individual for they are a natural endowment. But we can, in virtue of an increased emphasis, determine whether they shall be expressed in this or that direction. The love of adventure may, for example, be exhausted in the pursuit of some piratical enterprise, or it may be guided into channels of some useful form of social effort. It lies with society itself to see that the environment is such as to exercise a determining influence with regard to expressions of activity that are beneficial to the whole of the group.

To sum up. Evolution is no more than a formula that expresses the way in which a moving balance of forces is brought about by purely mechanical means. So far as animal life is concerned this balance is expressed by the phrase "adaptation to environment." But in human society the environment is in a growing measure made up of ideas, customs, traditions, ideals, and beliefs; in a word, of factors which are themselves products of human activities. And it is for this reason that the game of civilization is very largely in our own hands. If we maintain an environment in which it is either costly or dangerous to be honest and fearless in the expression of opinion, we shall be doing our best to develop mental cowardice and hypocrisy. If we bring up the young with the successful soldier or money-maker before them as examples, while we continue to treat the scientist as a crank, and the reformer as a dangerous criminal, we shall be continuing the policy of forcing the expression of human capacity on a lower level than would otherwise be the case. If we encourage the dominance of a religion which while making a profession of disinterested loftiness continues to irradiate a narrow egotism and a pessimistic view of life, we are doing our best to perpetuate an environment which emphasizes only the poorer aspects of human motive. Two centuries of ceaseless scientific activity have taught us something of the rules of the game which we are all playing with nature whether we will or no. To-day we have a good many of the winning cards in our hands, if we will only learn to play them wisely. It is not correct to say that evolution necessarily involves progress, but it does indicate that wisdom and foresight may so control the social forces as to turn that ceaseless change which is indicated by the law of evolution into channels that make for happiness and prosperity.

CHAPTER XII
DARWINISM AND DESIGN

The influence of the hypothesis of evolution on religion was not long in making itself felt. Professor Huxley explained the rapid success of Darwinism by saying that the scientific world was ready for it. And much the same thing may be said of the better representatives of the intellectual world with regard to the bearing of evolution on religion. In many directions the cultivated mind had for more than half a century been getting familiar with the general conception of growth in human life and thought. Where earlier generations had seen no more than a pattern to unravel there had developed a conviction that there was a history to trace and to understand. Distant parts of the world had been brought together during the seventeenth and the eighteenth centuries, readers and students were getting familiarized with the mass of customs and religious ideas that were possessed by these peoples, and it was perceived that beneath the bewildering variety of man's mental output there were certain features which they had in common, and which might hold in solution some common principle or principles.

This common principle was found in the conception of evolution. It was the one thing which, if true, and apart from the impossible idea of a revelation, nicely graduated to the capacities of different races, offered an explanation of the religions of the world in terms more satisfactory than those of deliberate invention or imposture. Once it was accepted, if only as an instrument of investigation, its use was soon justified. And the thorough-going nature of the conquest achieved is in no wise more clearly manifested than in the fact that the conception of growth is, to-day, not merely an accepted principle with scientific investigators, it has sunk deeply into all our literature and forms an unconscious part of popular thought.

One aspect of the influence of evolution on religious ideas has already been noted. It made the religious idea but one of the many forms that were assumed by man's attempt to reduce his experience of the world to something like an orderly theory. But that carried with it, for religion, the danger of reducing it to no more than one of the many theories of things which man forms, with the prospect of its rejection as a better knowledge of the world develops. Evolution certainly divested religion of any authority save such as it might contain in itself, and that is a position a religious mind can never contemplate with equanimity.

But so far as the theory of Darwinism is concerned it exerted a marked and rapid influence on the popular religious theory of design in nature. This is one of the oldest arguments in favour of a reasoned belief in God, and it is the one which was, and is still in one form or another, held in the greatest popular esteem. To the popular mind—and religion in a civilized country is not seriously concerned about its failing grip on the cultured intelligence so long as it keeps control of the ordinary man and woman—to the popular mind the argument from design appealed with peculiar force. Anyone is capable of admiring the wonders of nature, and in the earlier developments of popular science the marvels of plant and animal structures served only to deepen the Theist's admiration of the "divine wisdom." The examples of complexity of structure, of the interdependence of parts, and of the thousand and one cunning devices by which animal life maintains itself in the face of a hostile environment were there for all to see and admire. And when man compared these with his own conscious attempts to adapt means to ends, there seemed as strong proof here as anywhere of some scheming intelligence behind the natural process.

But the strength of the case was more apparent than real. It was weakest at the very point where it should have been strongest. In the case of a human product we know the purpose and can measure the extent of its realization in the nature of the result. In the case of a natural product we have no means of knowing what the purpose was, or even if any purpose at all lies behind the product. The important element in the argument from design—that of purpose—is thus pure assumption. In the case of human productions we argue from purpose to production. In the case of a natural object we are arguing from production to an assumed purpose. The analogy breaks down just where it should be strongest and clearest.

Now it is undeniable that to a very large number of the more thoughtful the old form of the argument from design received its death blow from the Darwinian doctrine of natural selection. In the light of this theory there was no greater need to argue that intelligence was necessary to produce animal adaptations than there was to assume intelligence for the sifting of sand by the wind. As the lighter grains are carried farthest because they are lightest, so natural selection, operating upon organic variations, favoured the better adapted specimens by killing off the less favoured ones. The fittest is not created, it survives. The world is not what it is because the animal is what it is, the animal is what it is because the world is as it is. It cannot be any different and live—a truth demonstrated by the destruction of myriads of animal forms, and by the disappearance of whole species. The case was so plain, the evidence so conclusive, that the clearer headed religionists dropped the old form of the argument from design as no longer tenable.

But the gentleman who exchanged the errors of the Church of Rome for those of the Church of England is always with us. And the believer in deity having dropped the argument from design in one form immediately proceeded to revive it in another. This was, perhaps, inevitable. After all, man lives in this world, and if proof of the existence of deity is to be gathered from his works, it must be derived from the world we know. So design *must* be found somewhere, and it must be found here. Only one chance was left. The general hypothesis of evolution—either Darwinism alone, or Darwinism plus other factors—explained the development of animal life. But that was *within* the natural process. What, then, of the process as a whole? If the hand of God could not be seen in the particular adaptations of animal life, might it not be that the whole of the process, in virtue of which these particular adaptations occurred, might be the expression of the divine intelligence? God did not create the particular parts directly, but may he not have created the whole, leaving it for the forces he had set in motion to work out his "plan." The suggestion was attractive. It relieved religion from resting its case in a region where proof and disproof are possible, and removed it to a region where they are difficult, if not impossible. So, as it was not possible to uphold the old teleology, one began to hear a great deal of the "wider teleology," which meant that the Theist was thinking vaguely when he imagined he was thinking comprehensively, and that, because he had reached a region where the laws of logic could not be applied, he concluded that he had achieved demonstration. And, indeed, when one gets outside the region of verification there is nothing to stop one theorizing— save a dose of common-sense and a gracious gift of humour.

In another work (*Theism or Atheism*) I have dealt at length with the argument from design. At present my aim is to take the presentation of this "wider teleology" as given by a well-known writer on philosophical subjects, Mr. F. C. S. Schiller, in a volume published a few years ago entitled *Humanism: Philosophical Essays*. And in doing so, it is certain that the theologian will lose nothing by leaving himself in the hands of so able a representative.

Mr. Schiller naturally accepts Darwinism as at least an important factor in organic evolution, but he does not believe that it excludes design, and he does believe that "our attitude towards life will be very different, according as we believe it to be inspired and guided by intelligence or hold it to be the fortuitous product of blind mechanisms, whose working our helpless human intelligence can observe, but cannot control."

Now within its scope Darwinism certainly does exclude design, and even though the forces represented by natural selection may be directed towards the end produced, yet so far as the play of these forces is concerned they are really self-directing, or self-contained. The argument really seems to be just mere theology masquerading as philosophy. Theories do play some part in the determination of the individual attitude towards life, but they do not play the important part that Mr. Schiller assumes they play. It is easily observable that the same theory of life held by a Christian in England and by another Christian in Asia Minor has, so far as it affects conduct, different results. And if it be said that even though the results be different they are still there, the reply is that they differ because the facts of life compel an adjustment in terms of the general environment. Mr. Schiller admits that the "prevalent conduct and that adapted to the conditions of life must coincide," and the admission is fatal to his position. The truth of the matter is that the conditions of life being what they are, and the consequences of conduct being also what they are, speculative theories of life cannot, in the nature of the case, affect life beyond a certain point; that is, if life is to continue. That is why in the history of belief religious teachings have sooner or later to accommodate themselves to persistent facts.

Mr. Schiller brings forward two arguments in favour of reconciling Darwinism and Design, both of them ingenious, but neither of them conclusive. With both of these I will deal later; but it is first necessary to notice one or two of his arguments against a non-Theistic Darwinism. The denial of the argument from design, he says, leads farther than most people imagine:—

> A complete denial of design in nature must deny the efficacy of all intelligence as such. A consistently mechanical view has to regard all intelligence as otiose, as an "epi-phenomenal by-product" or fifth wheel to the cart, in the absence of which the given results would no less have occurred. And so, if this view were the truth, we should have to renounce all effort to direct our fated and ill-fated course down the stream of time. Our consciousness would be an unmeaning accident.

A complete reply to this would involve an examination of the meaning that is and ought to be attached to "intelligence," and that is too lengthy an enquiry to be attempted here. It is, perhaps, enough to point out that Mr. Schiller's argument clearly moves on the assumption that intelligence is a *thing* or a quality which exists, so to speak, in its own right and which interferes with the course of events as something from without. It is quite probable that he would repudiate this construction being placed on his words, but if he does not mean that, then I fail to see what he does mean, or what force there is in his argument. And it is enough for my purpose to point out that "intelligence" or mind is not a thing, but a relation. It asserts of a certain class of actions exactly what "gravitation" asserts of a certain class of motion, and "thingness" is no more asserted in the one case than it is in the other.

Intelligence, as a name given to a special class of facts or actions, remains, whatever view we take of its nature, and it is puzzling to see why the denial of extra natural intelligence—that is, intelligence separated from all the conditions under which we know the phenomenon of intelligence—should be taken as involving the denial of the existence of intelligence as we know it. Intelligence as connoting purposive action remains as much a fact as gravity or chemical attraction, and continues valid concerning the phenomena it is intended to cover. All that the evolutionist is committed to is the statement that it is as much a product of evolution as is the shape or colouring of animals. It is not at all a question of self-dependence. Every force in nature must be taken for what it is worth, intelligence among them. Why, then, does the view that intelligence is both a product of evolution and a cause of another phase of evolution land us in self-contradiction, or make the existence of itself meaningless? The truth is that intelligence determines results exactly as every other force in nature determines results, by acting as a link in an unending sequential chain. And the question as to what intelligence is *per se* is as meaningless as what gravitation is *per se*. These are names which we give to groups of phenomena displaying particular and differential characteristics, and their purpose is served when they enable us to cognize and recognize these phenomena and to give them their place and describe their function in the series of changes that make up our world.

Mr. Schiller's reply to this line of criticism is the familiar one that it reduces human beings to automata. He says:—

> The ease with which the Darwinian argument dispenses
> with intelligence as a factor in survival excites suspicion. It
> is proving too much to show that adaptation might equally
> well have arisen in automata. For we ourselves are strongly
> persuaded that we are not automata and strive hard to adapt
> ourselves. In us at least, therefore, intelligence *is* a source of
> adaptation.... Intelligence therefore is a *vera causa* as a source
> of adaptations at least co-ordinate with Natural Selection,
> and this can be denied only if it is declared inefficacious
> *everywhere*; if all living beings, including ourselves, are
> declared to be automata.

One is compelled again to point out that Darwinism does not dispense with intelligence as a factor in survival, except so far as the intelligence which determines survival is declared to be operating apart from the organisms which survive. The conduct of one of the lower animals which reacts only to the immediate promptings of its environment is of one order, but the response of another animal not merely to the immediate promptings of the environment, but to remote conditions, as in the selection of food or the building of a home of some sort, or to the fashioning of a tool, does obviously give to the intelligence displayed a distinct survival value. And that effectively replies to the triumphant conclusion, "If intelligence has no efficacy in promoting adaptations, *i.e.*, if it has no survival value, how comes it to be developed at all?"

Darwinism would never have been able to dispense with intelligence in the way it did but for the fact that the opposite theory never stood for more than a mere collection of words. That species are or were produced by the operations of "Divine Intelligence" is merely a grandiloquent way of saying nothing at all. It is absurd to pretend that such a formula ever had any scientific value. It explains nothing. And it is quite obvious that some adaptations do, so far as we know, arise without intelligence, and are, therefore, to use Mr. Schiller's expression, automata. (I do not like the word, since it conveys too much the notion of someone behind the scenes pulling strings.) And it is on his theory that animals actually are automata. For if there be a "Divine mind" which stands as the active cause of the adaptations that meet us in the animal world, and who arranges forces so that they shall work to their pre-destined end, what is that but converting the whole of the animal world into so many automata. One does not escape determinism in this way; it is only getting rid of it in one direction in order to reintroduce it in another.

And one would like to know what our conviction that we are not automata has to do with it. Whether the most rigid determinism is true or not is a matter to be settled by an examination of the facts and a careful reflection as to their real significance. No one questions that there is a persuasion to the contrary; if there were not there would be nothing around which controversy could gather. But it is the conviction that is challenged, and it is idle to reply to the challenge by asserting a conviction to the contrary. The whole history of human thought is the record of a challenge and a reversal of such convictions. There never was a conviction which was held more strenuously than that the earth was flat. The experience of all men in every hour of their lives seemed to prove it. And yet to-day no one believes it. The affirmation that we are "free" rests, as Spinoza said, ultimately on the fact that all men know their actions and but few know the causes thereof. A feather endowed with consciousness, falling to the ground in a zigzag manner, might be equally convinced that it determined the exact spot on which it would rest, yet its persuasion would be of no more value than the "vulgar" conviction that we independently adapt ourselves to our environment.

Mr. Schiller's positive arguments in favour of reconciling Darwinism with design—one of them is really negative;—are concerned with (1) the question of variation, and (2) with the existence of progress. On the first question it is pointed out that while Natural Selection operates by way of favouring certain variations, the origin or cause of these variations remains unknown. And although Mr. Schiller does not say so in as many words, there is the implication, if I rightly discern his drift, that there is room here for a directing intelligence, inasmuch as science is at present quite unable to fully explain the causes of variations. We are told that Darwin assumed for the purpose of his theory that variations were indefinite both as to character and extent, and it is upon these variations that Natural Selection depends. This indefinite variation Mr. Schiller asserts to be a methodological device, that is, it is something assumed as the groundwork of a theory, but without any subsequent verification, and it is in virtue of this assumption that intelligence is ruled out of evolution. And inasmuch as Mr. Schiller sees no reason for believing that variations are of this indefinite character, he asserts that there is in evolution room for a teleological factor, in other words, "a purposive direction of variations."

Now it hardly needs pointing out to students of Darwinism that indefinite variation is the equivalent of "a variation to which no exact limits can be placed," and in this sense the assumption is a perfectly sound one. From one point of view the variations must be definite, that is, they can only occur within certain limits. An elephant will not vary in the direction of wings, nor will a bird in the direction of a rose bush. But so long as we cannot fix the exact limits of variation we are quite warranted in speaking of them as indefinite. That this is a methodological device no one denies, but so are most of the other distinctions that we frame. Scientific generalizations consist of abstractions, and Mr. Schiller himself of necessity employs the same device.

Mr. Schiller argues, quite properly, that while Natural Selection states the conditions under which animal life evolves, it does not state any reason why it should evolve. Selection may keep a species stationary or it may even cause it to degenerate. Both are fairly common phenomena in the animal and plant world. Moreover, if there are an indefinite number of variations, and if they tend in an indefinite number of directions, then the variation in any one direction can never be more than an infinitesimal portion of the whole, and that this one should persist supplies a still further reason for belief in "a purposive direction of variations." Mr. Schiller overlooks an important point here, but a very simple one. It is true that any one variation is small in relation to the whole of the possible or actual number of variations. But it is not in relation to quantity but quality that survival takes place, and in proportion to the keenness of the struggle the variation that gives its possessor an advantage need only be of the smaller kind. In a struggle of endurance between two athletes it is the one capable of holding out for an extra minute who carries off the prize.

Further, as Mr. Schiller afterwards admits, the very smallness of the number of successful variations makes against intelligence rather than for it, and he practically surrenders his position in the statement, "the teleological and anti-teleological interpretation of events will ever decide their conflict by appealing to the facts; for in the facts each finds what it wills and comes prepared to see." After this lame conclusion it is difficult to see what value there is in Mr. Schiller's own examination of the "facts." Not that it is strictly correct to say that the facts bear each view out equally. They do not, and Mr. Schiller only justifies his statement by converting the Darwinian position, which is teleologically negative, into an affirmative. The Darwinian, he says, denies intelligence as a cause of evolution. What the Darwinian does is to deny the validity of the evidence which the teleologist brings to prove his case. The Theist asserts mind as a cause of evolution. The Darwinian simply points out that the facts may be explained in quite another way and without the appeal to a quite unknown factor.

And here one might reasonably ask, why, if there is a directive mind at work, are there variations at all? Why should the "directive intelligence" not get earlier to work, and instead of waiting until a large number of specimens have been produced and then looking them over with a view to "directing" the preservation of the better specimens, why should it not set to work at the beginning and see that only the desirable ones make their appearance? Certainly that is what a mere human intelligence would do if it could. But it is characteristic of the "Divine Intelligence" of the Theist that it never seems to operate with a tenth part of the intelligence of an ordinary human being.

Moreover, Mr. Schiller writes quite ignoring the fact that the "directive intelligence" does not direct the preservation of the better specimens. What it does, if it does anything at all, is to kill off the less favoured ones. Natural Selection—the point is generally overlooked by the Theistic sentimentality of most of our writers—does not preserve anything. Its positive action is not to keep alive but to kill. It does not take the better ones in hand and help them. It seizes on all it can and kills them. It is the difference between a local council that tried to raise the standard of health by a general improvement of the conditions of life, and one that aimed at the same end by killing off all children that failed to come up to a certain standard. The actual preservation of a better type is, so far as Natural Selection is concerned, quite accidental. So far as Natural Selection operates it does so by elimination, not by preservation.

Mr. Schiller's other plea in favour of Design is concerned with the conception of progress. He points out that while degeneration and stagnation both occur in nature, yet—

> life has been on the whole progressive; but progress and retrogression have both been effected under the same law of Natural Selection. How, then, can the credit of that result be ascribed to Natural Selection? Natural Selection is equally ready to bring about degeneration or to leave things unchanged. How, then, can it be that which determines which of the three possible (and actual) cases shall be realized?... It cannot be Natural Selection that causes one species to remain stationary, another to degenerate, a third to develop into a higher form.... Some variable factor must be added to Natural Selection.

But why? Evolution, as we have pointed out in a previous chapter, makes for adaptation in terms of animal preservation. If the adaptation of an animal to its environment is secured by "degenerating" or "developing" or by remaining stationary, it will do one of the three. That is the normal consequence of Natural Selection, and it is surprising that Mr. Schiller does not see this. He is actually accusing Natural Selection of not being able to do what it does on his own showing. The proof he himself gives of this operation of Natural Selection in the examples he cites of its ineffectiveness. If Natural Selection could not make for degeneration or development, in what way would it be able to establish an equilibrium between an animal and its surroundings? Really, there is nothing that so strengthens one's conviction of the truth of the Freethought position so much as a study of the arguments that are brought against it.

Mr. Schiller is really misled, and so misleads his readers by an unjustifiable use of the word "progress." He says that evolution has been, on the whole, progressive, and appeals to "progress" as though it were some objective fact. But that is not the case. There is no "progress" in the animal world, there is only change. We have dealt with this in a previous chapter, and there is no need to again labour the point. "Progress" is a conception which we ourselves frame, and we measure a movement towards or away from this arbitrary standard of ours in terms of better or worse, higher or lower. But nature knows nothing of a higher or a lower, it knows only of changing forms more or less fitted to live in the existing environment. Scientifically, life has not progressed, it has persisted, and a *sine qua non* of its persistence has been adaptation to environment.

Progress, then, is not a "natural" fact, but a methodological one. It is a useful word and a valuable ideal. I am not protesting against its use, only against its misuse. It is one of the many abstractions created by thinkers, and then worshipped as a reality by those who forget the origin and purpose of its existence. And in this we can see one of the fatal legacies we have inherited from Theistic methods of thinking. The belief that things are designed to be as they are comes to us from those primitive methods of thinking which personify and vitalize all natural phenomena. We have outgrown the crude frame of mind which saw direct volitional action in a storm or in the movements of natural forces. The development of civilized and scientific thinking has removed these conceptions from the minds of educated men and women, but it has left behind it as a residuum the habit of looking for purpose where none exists, and of reading into nature as objective facts our own generalizations and abstractions. And so long as we have not outgrown that habit we are retaining a fatal bar to exact scientific thinking.

Finally, and this consideration is fatal to any theory of design such as Mr. Schiller champions, adaptation is not a special quality of one form of existence, but a universal quality of all. There is not a greater degree of adaptation here and a less degree there, but the same degree in every case. There is no other meaning to adaptation except that of adjustment to surroundings. But whether an animal lives or dies, whether it is higher or lower, deformed or perfect, the adjustment is the same. That is, every form of existence represents the product of forces that have made it what it is, and the same forces could not have produced anything different. Every body in existence, organic or inorganic, constitutes in ultimate analysis a balance of the forces represented by it. It is not possible, therefore, for the Theist to say that design is evidenced by adaptation in one case and its absence in another. There is adaptation in every case, even though it may not be the adaptation we should like to see. It is not possible for the Theist to say that the *degree* of adaptation is greater in the one case than in the other, for *that* is the same in every case. What needs to be done if design is to be established is to prove that the forces we see at work could not have produced the results that emerge without the introduction of a factor not already given in our experience. Anything else is mere waste of time.

CHAPTER XIII
ANCIENT AND MODERN

In the preceding chapters we have, without saying it in so many words, been emphasizing the modern as against the ancient point of view. The distinction may not at first glance appear to be of great moment, and yet reflection will prove it to be of vital significance. It expresses, in a sentence, the essence of the distinction between the Freethinker and the religionist. Objectively, the world in which we are living is the same as that in which our ancestors lived. The same stars that looked down upon them look down upon us. Natural forces affected them as they affect us. Even the play of human passion and desire was the same with them as with us. Hunger and thirst, love and hatred, cowardice and courage, generosity and greed operate now as always. The world remains the same in all its essential features; what alters is our conception of it—in other words, the point of view.

The question thus resolves itself into one of interpretation. Freethinker and religionist are each living in the same world, they are each fed with the same foods and killed with the same poisons. The same feelings move both and the same problems face both. Their differences are constituted by the canon of interpretation applied. It is on this issue that the conflict between religion and science arises. For religion is not, as some have argued, something that is supplementary or complementary to science, nor does it deal with matters on which science is incompetent to express an opinion. Religion and science face each other as rival interpretations of the same set of facts, precisely as the Copernican and the Ptolemaic systems once faced each other as rival interpretations of astronomical phenomena. If the one is true the other is false. You may reject the religious or the scientific explanation of phenomena, but you cannot logically accept both. As Dr. Johnson said, "Two contradictory ideas may inhere in the same mind, but they cannot both be correct."

Now while it is true that in order to understand the present we must know the past, and that because the present is a product of the past, it is also true that a condition of understanding is to interpret the past by the present. In ordinary affairs this is not questioned. When geologists set out to explain the causes of changes in the earth's surface, they utilize the present-day knowledge of existing forces, and by prolonging their action backward explain the features of the period they are studying. When historians seek to explain the conduct of, say Henry the Eighth, they take their knowledge of the motives animating existing human nature, and by placing that in a sixteenth century setting manage to present us with a picture of the period. So, again, when the thirteenth century monkish historian gravely informs us that a particular epidemic was due to the anger of God against the wickedness of the people, we put that interpretation on one side and use our own knowledge to find in defective social and sanitary conditions the cause of what occurred. Illustrations to the same end may be found in every direction. It is, indeed, not something that one may accept or reject as one may take or leave a political theory, it is an indispensible condition of rational thinking on any subject whatsoever.

Accepted everywhere else, it is in connection with religion that one finds this principle, not openly challenged, for there are degrees of absurdity to which even the most ardent religionist dare not go, but it is quietly set on one side and a method adopted which is its practical negation. Either the procedure is inverted and the present is interpreted by the past, as when it is assumed that because God did certain things in the past therefore he will continue to do the same things in the present, or it is assumed that the past was unlike the present, and, therefore, the same method of interpretation cannot be applied to both cases. Both plans have the effect of landing us, if not in lunacy, at least well on the way to it.

It is indispensible to the religionist to ignore the principle above laid down. For if it is admitted that human nature is always and everywhere the same, and that natural forces always and everywhere act in the same manner, religious beliefs are brought to the test of their conformity with present day knowledge of things and all claim to objective validity must be abandoned. Yet the principle is quite clear. The claim of the prophets of old to be inspired must be tested by what we know of the conditions of "inspiration" to-day, and not by what unenlightened people thought of its nature centuries ago. Whether the story of the Virgin Birth is credible or not must be settled by an appeal to what we know of the nature of animal procreation, and not by whether our faith urges us to accept the statement as true. To act otherwise is to raise an altogether false issue, the question of evidence is argued when what is really at issue is that of credibility. It is not at all a matter of whether there is evidence enough to establish the reality of a particular recorded event, but whether our actual knowledge of natural happenings is not enough for us to rule it out as objectively untrue, and to describe the conditions which led to its being accepted as true.

Let us take as an illustration of this the general question of miracles. The *Oxford Dictionary* defines a miracle as "A marvellous event occurring within human experience which cannot have been brought about by human power or by the operation of any natural agency, and must, therefore, be ascribed to the special intervention of the deity or some supernatural being." That is a good enough definition, and is certainly what people have had in mind when they have professed a belief in miracles. A miracle must be something marvellous, that is, it must be unusual, and it must not be even conceivably explainable in terms of the operation of natural forces. If it is admitted that what is claimed as a miracle might be explained as the result of natural forces provided our knowledge was extensive enough and exact enough, it is confessed that miracle and ignorance are convertible terms. And while that may be true enough as a matter of fact, it would never suit the religious case to admit it in so many words.

Nor would it make the case any better to argue that the alleged miracle has been brought about by some superior being with a much greater knowledge of nature than man possesses, but which the latter may one day acquire. That is placing a miracle on the same level as a performance given by a clever conjuror, which puzzles the onlooker because he lacks the technical knowledge requisite to understand the methods employed. A miracle to be a miracle must not be in accordance with natural laws, known or unknown, it must contravene them or suspend their operation.

On the other hand, the demand made by some critics of the miraculous, namely, that the alleged miracle shall be performed under test conditions, is absurd, and shows that they have not grasped the essential point at issue. The believer's reply to such a demand is plain and obvious. He says, a miracle is by its nature a rare event, it is performed under special circumstances to serve a special purpose. Where, then, is the reason in asking that this miracle shall be re-performed in order to convince certain people that it has already occurred? To arrange for the performance of a miracle is an absurdity. For it to become common is to destroy both its character as a miracle and the justification for its existence. A miracle must carry its own evidence or it fails of its purpose and ceases to be a miracle at all. Discussion on these lines ends, at best, in a stalemate.

It is just as wide of the mark to discuss miracles as though it were a question of evidence. What possible evidence could there be, for example, that Jesus fed five thousand people with a few loaves and fishes, and had basketfuls left at the end of the repast? Suppose it were possible to produce the sworn testimony of the five thousand themselves that they had been so fed. Would that produce conviction? Would it do any more than prove that they believed the food had been so expanded or multiplied that it was enough for them all? It would be convincing, perhaps, as proof of an act of belief. But would it prove any more than that? Would it prove that these five thousand were not the victims of some act of deception or of some delusion? A belief in a miracle, whether the belief dates from two thousand years since or from last week, proves only—belief. And the testimony of a Salvation Army convert as to the truth of the resurrection of Jesus Christ is as good, as evidence, as though we had the sworn testimony of the twelve apostles, with that of the grave-diggers thrown in.

The truth is that the question of belief in the miraculous has nothing whatever to do with evidence. Miracles are never established by evidence, nor are they disproved by evidence, that is, so long as we use the term evidence with any regard to its judicial significance. What amount or what kind of evidence did the early Christians require to prove the miracles of Christianity? Or what evidence did our ancestors require to prove to them that old women flew through the air on broomsticks, or bewitched cows, or raised storms? Testimony in volumes was forthcoming, and there is not the slightest reason for doubting its genuineness. But what amount or kind of evidence was required to establish the belief? Was it evidence to which anyone to-day would pay the slightest regard? The slightest study of the available records is enough to show that the question of evidence had nothing whatever to do with the production of the belief.

And, on the other hand, how many people have given up the belief in miracles as a result of a careful study of the evidence against them? I have never heard of any such case, although once a man disbelieves in miracles he may be ready enough to produce reasons to justify his disbelief in them. The man who begins to weigh evidence for and against miracles has already begun to disbelieve them.

The attitude of children in relation to the belief in fairies may well be taken to illustrate the attitude of the adult mind in face of the miraculous. No evidence is produced to induce the belief in fairies, and none is ever brought forward to induce them to give it up. At one stage of life it is there, at another it is gone. It is not reasoned out or evidenced out, it is simply outgrown. In infancy the child's conception of life is so inchoate that there is room for all kinds of fantastic beliefs. In more mature years certain beliefs are automatically ruled out by the growth of a conception of things which leaves no room for beliefs that during childhood seemed perfectly reasonable.

Now this is quite on all-fours with the question of miracles. The issue is essentially one of psychology. Belief or disbelief is here mainly determined by the psychological medium in which one lives and moves. Given a psychological medium which is, scientifically, at its lowest, and the belief in the miraculous flourishes. At the other extreme miracles languish and decay. Tell a savage that the air is alive with good and bad spirits and he will readily believe you. Tell it to a man with a genuine scientific mind and he will laugh at you. Tell a peasant in some parts of the country that someone is a witch and he will at once believe it. Tell it to a city dweller and it will provide only occasion for ridicule. People who accept miracles believe them before they happen. The expressed belief merely registers the fact. Miracles never happen to those who do not believe in them; as has been said, they never occur to a critic. Those who reject miracles do so because their acceptance would conflict with their whole conception of nature. That is the sum and substance of the matter.

A further illustration may be offered in the case of the once much debated question of the authenticity of the books of the New Testament and the historicity of the figure of Jesus. It appears to have been assumed that if it could be shown that the books of the New Testament were not contemporary records the case against the divinity of Jesus was strengthened. On the other hand it was assumed that if these writings represented the narratives of contemporaries the case for the truth of the narratives was practically proven. In reality this was not the vital issue at all. It would be, of course, interesting if it could be shown that there once existed an actual personage around whom these stories gathered, but it would make as little difference to the real question at issue as the demonstration of the Baconian authorship of *Hamlet* would make in the psychological value of the play.

Suppose then it were proven that a person named Jesus actually existed at a certain date in Judea, and that this person is the Jesus of the New Testament. Suppose it be further proven, or admitted, that the followers whom this person gathered around him believed that he was born of a virgin, performed a number of miracles, was crucified, and then rose from the dead, and that the New Testament represents their written memoirs. Suppose all this to be proven or granted, what has been established? Simply this. That a number of people believed these things of someone whom they had known. But no Freethinker need seriously concern himself to disprove this. He may, indeed, take it as the data of the problem which he sets out to solve. The scientific enquirer is not really concerned with the New Testament as a narrative of fact any more than he is concerned with Cotton Mather's *Invisible World Displayed* as a narrative of actual fact. What he is concerned with is the frame of mind to which these stories seemed true, and the social medium which gave such a frame of mind a vogue. It is not at all a question of historical evidence, but of historical psychology. It is not a question of the honesty of the witnesses, but of their ability, not whether they wished to tell the truth, or intended to tell the truth, but whether they were in a position to know what the truth was. We have not to discuss whether these events occurred, such a proposition is an insult to a civilized intelligence, the matter for discussion is the conditions that bring such beliefs into existence and the conditions that perpetuate them.

The development of social life and of education thus shifts the point of view from the past to the present. To understand the past we do not ask what was it that people believed concerning the events around them, but what do we know of the causes which produce beliefs of a certain kind. Thus, we do not really reject the story of Jesus turning water into wine because we are without legal evidence that he ever did anything of the kind, but because, knowing the chemical constituents of both water and wine we know that such a thing is impossible. It is only possible to an uninstructed mind to which water and wine differ only in taste or appearance. We do not reject the story of the demoniacs in the New Testament because we have no evidence that these men were possessed of devils, or that Jesus cast them out, but because we have exactly the same phenomena with us to-day and know that it comes within the province of the physician and not of the miracle worker. It is not a matter of evidence whether a man rose from the dead or not, or whether he was born of a virgin or not, but solely a question of examining these and similar stories in the light of present day knowledge. The "evidence" offered is proof only of belief, and no one ever questioned the existence of that. And if the proof of belief is required there is no need to go back a couple of thousand years or to consult ancient records. The testimony of a present day believer, and the account of a revival meeting such as one may find in any religious newspaper will serve equally well. As is so often the case, the evidence offered is not merely inadequate, it is absolutely irrelevant.

Past events must be judged in the light of present knowledge. That is the golden rule of guidance in judging the world's religious legends. And that canon is fatal to their pretensions. On the one hand we see in the life of contemporary savages and in that of semi-civilized peoples all the conditions and the beliefs that meet us in the Bible and among the early Christians. And with our wider and more exact knowledge we are able to take exactly the same phenomena that impressed those of an earlier generation and explain them without the slightest reference to supernatural powers or beings. The modern mind is really not looking round for evidence to disprove the truth of Christian legends. It knows they are not true. There is no greater need to prove that the miracles of Christianity never occurred, than there is to prove that an old woman never raised a storm to wreck one of the kings of England. The issue has been changed from one of history to one of psychology. It is the present that of necessity sits in judgment on the past, and it is in the light of the knowledge of the present that the religions of the past stand condemned.

CHAPTER XIV
MORALITY WITHOUT GOD

The mystery-monger flourishes almost as well in ethics as he does in theology. Indeed, in some respects he seems to have forsaken one field of exercise only to find renewed scope in the other. He approaches the consideration of moral questions with the same hushed voice and "reverential" air that is so usual in theology, and talks of the mystery of morality with the same facility that he once talked about the mystery of godliness—and with about an equal amount of enlightenment to his hearers or readers.

But the mystery of morality is nearly all of our own making. Essentially there is no more mystery in morality than there is in any other question that may engage the attention of mankind. There are, of course, problems in the moral world as there are in the physical one, and he would be a fool who pretended to the ability to satisfactorily solve them all. The nature of morality, the causes that led to the development of moral "laws," and still more to the development of a sense of morality, all these are questions upon which there is ample room for research and speculation. But the talk of a mystery is misleading and mystifying. It is the chatter of the charlatan, or of the theologian, or of the partly liberated mind that is still under the thraldom of theology. In ethics we have exactly the same kind of problem that meets us in any of the sciences. We have a fact, or a series of facts, and we seek some explanation of them. We may fail in our search, but that is not evidence of a "mystery," it is proof only of inadequate knowledge, of limitations that we may hope the future will enable us to overcome.

For the sake of clarity it will be better to let the meaning of morality emerge from the discussion rather than to commence with it. And one of the first things to help to clear the mind of confusion is to get rid of the notion that there is any such thing as moral "laws" which correspond in their nature to law as the term is used in science. In one sense morality is not part of physical nature at all. It is characteristic of that part of nature which is covered by the human—at most by the higher animal—world. Nature can only, therefore, be said to be moral in the sense that the term "Nature" includes all that is. In any other sense nature is non-moral. The sense of values, which is, as we shall see, of the essence of the conception of morality, nature knows nothing of. To speak of nature punishing us for *bad* actions or rewarding us for *good* ones is absurd. Nature neither punishes nor rewards. She meets actions with consequences, and is quite indifferent to any moral consideration. If I am weakly, and go out on a cold, wet night to help someone in distress, nature does not act differently than it would if I had gone out to commit a murder. I stand exactly the same chances in either case of contracting a deadly chill. It is not the moral value of an action with which natural forces are concerned, but merely with the action, and in that respect nature never discriminates between the good man and the bad, between the sinner and the saint.

There is another sense in which moral laws differ from natural laws. We can break the former but not the latter. The expression so often used, "He broke a law of nature," is absurd. You cannot break a law of nature. You do not break the law of gravitation when you prevent a stone falling to the ground; the force required to hold it in the air is an illustration of the law. It is, indeed, one of the proofs that our generalization does represent a law of nature that it cannot be "broken." For broken is here only another word for inoperative, and a law of nature that is inoperative is non-existent. But in the moral sphere we are in a different world. We not only can break moral laws, we do break them; that is one of the problems with which our teachers and moralisers have constantly to deal. Every time we steal we break the law "Thou shalt not steal." Every time we murder we break the law "Thou shalt not kill." We may keep moral laws, we ought to keep them, but we can, quite clearly, break them. Between a moral law and a law of nature there is plainly a very radical distinction. The discovery of that distinction will, I think, bring us to the heart of the subject.

Considering man as merely a natural object, or as a mere animal, there is only one quality that nature demands of him. This is efficiency. Nature's sole law is here "Be Strong." How that strength and efficiency is secured and maintained is of no consequence whatever. The heat he requires, the food he needs may be stolen from others, but it will serve. The food will not nourish the less, the fire will not warm the less. So long as efficiency is acquired it is a matter of absolute indifference how it is secured. Considered as a mere animal object it is difficult to see that morality has any meaning at all for man. It is when we come to regard him in his relation to others that we begin to see the meaning and significance of morality emerge.

Now one of the first things that strike us in connection with moral laws or rules is that they are all statements of relation. Such moral commands as "Thou shalt not steal," "Thou shalt not kill," the commands to be truthful, kind, dutiful, etc., all imply a relation to others. Apart from this relation moral rules have simply no meaning whatever. By himself a man could neither steal, nor lie, nor do any of the things that we habitually characterize as immoral. A man living by himself on some island would be absolved from all moral law; it would have no meaning whatever for him. He would be neither moral nor immoral, he would simply be without the conditions that make morality possible. But once bring him into relations with his kind and his behaviour begins to have a new and peculiar significance, not alone to these others, but also to himself. What he does affects them, and also affects himself so far as they determine the character of his relations to these others. He must, for example, either work with them or apart from them. He must either be on his guard against their securing their own efficiency at his expense, or rest content that a mutual forbearance and trust will govern their association. To ignore them is an impossibility. He must reckon with these others in a thousand and one different ways, and this reckoning will have its effect on the moulding of his nature and upon theirs.

Morality, then, whatever else it may be, is primarily the expression of a relation. And the laws of morality are, consequently, a summary or description of those relations. From this point of view they stand upon exactly the same level as any of the arts or sciences. Moral actions are the subject matter of observation, and the determination of their essential quality or character is by the same methods as we determine the essential quality of the "facts" in chemistry or biology. The task before the scientific enquirer is, therefore, to determine the conditions which give to moral rules or "laws" their meaning and validity.

One of the conditions of a moral action has already been pointed out. This is that all moral rules imply a relation to beings of a similar nature. A second feature is that conduct represents a form of efficiency, it is a special feature of the universal biological fact of adaptation. And the question of why man has a "moral sense" is really on all fours with, and presents no greater mystery than is involved in, the question of why man has digestive organs, and prefers some kinds of food to others. Substantially, the question of why man should prefer a diet of meat and potatoes to one of prussic acid is exactly the question of why society should discourage certain actions and encourage others, or why man's moral taste should prefer some forms of conduct to other forms. The answer to both questions, while differing in form, is the same in substance.

Man as we know him is always found as a member of a group, and his capacities, his feelings, and tastes must always be considered in relation to that fact. But considering man merely as an animal, and his conduct as merely a form of adaptation to environment, the plain consideration which emerges is that even as an individual organism he is compelled, in order to live, to avoid certain actions and to perform others, to develop certain tastes and to form certain distastes. To take our previous illustration it would be impossible for man to develop a liking for life-destroying foods. It is one of the conditions of living that he shall eat only that food which sustains life, or that he shall abstain from eating substances which destroy it. But conduct at that stage is not of the kind which considers the reasons for acting; indeed, life cannot be based upon considered action, however much reason may justify the actions taken. Further, as all conscious action is prompted by the impulse to do what is pleasant and to avoid what is unpleasant, it follows, as Spencer pointed out, that the course of evolution sets up a close relation between actions that are pleasurable in the performance and actions that are life preserving. It is one of the conditions of the maintenance of life that the pleasurable and the beneficial shall in the long run coincide.

When we take man as a member of a group we have the same principle in operation, even though the form of its expression undergoes alteration. To begin with, the mere fact of living in a group implies the growth of a certain restraint in one's relations to, and of reciprocity in dealing with, others. Men can no more live together without some amount of trust and confidence in each other, or without a crude sense of justice in their dealings with each other, than an individual man can maintain his life by eating deadly poisons. There must be a respect for the rights of others, of justice in dealing with others, and of confidence in associating with others, at least to the extent of not threatening the possibility of group life. There are rules in the game of social life that must be observed, and in its own defence society is bound to suppress those of its members who exhibit strong anti-social tendencies. No society can, for example, tolerate homicide as an admitted practice. There is, thus, from the earliest times, a certain form of elimination of the anti-social character which results in the gradual formation of an emotional and mental disposition that habitually and instinctively falls into line with the requirements of the social whole.

To use an expression of Sir Leslie Stephen's, man as a member of the group becomes a cell in the social tissue, and his fitness to survive is dependent upon, positively, his readiness to perform such actions as the welfare of the group require, and, negatively, upon his refraining from doing those things that are inimical to social welfare.[23] Moreover, there is the additional fact that the group itself is, as a whole, brought into contact with other groups, and the survival of one group as against another is determined by the quality and the degree of cohesion of its units. From this point of view, participation in the life of the group means more than refraining from acts that are injurious to the group, it involves some degree of positive contribution to social welfare.

But the main thing to note is that from the very dawn of animal life the organism is more or less under the pressure of a certain discipline that tends to establish an identity between actions which there is a tendency to perform and those that are beneficial to the organism. In the social state we simply have this principle expressed in another way, and it gives a degree of conscious adaptation that is absent from the pre-social or even the lower forms of the social state. It is in the truly social state also that we get the full influence of what may be called the characteristically human environment, that is, the operation of ideas and ideals. The importance of this psychological factor in the life of man has been stressed in an earlier chapter. It is enough now to point out that from the earliest moment the young human being is, by a process of training, imbued with certain ideals of truthfulness, loyalty, duty, etc., all of which play their part in the moulding of his character. However much these ideals may vary in different societies, the fact of the part played by them in moulding character is plain. They are the dominant forces in moulding the individual to the social state, even while the expressions of the social life may be in turn checked by the fact that social conduct cannot persist if it threatens those conditions upon which the persistence of life ultimately depends.

There is one other consideration that must be noted. One very pregnant fact in life is that nature seldom creates a new organ. What it usually does is to refashion an old one, or to devote an old one to new uses. This principle may be seen clearly in operation in connection with moral evolution. On the one hand the various forces that play upon human nature drive the moral feelings deeper into it. On the other hand it develops them by their steady expansion over a wider area. Whether it is an actual fact or not—I do not stress it because the point is the subject of discussion—it is at least possible that the earliest human group is the family. And so long as that was the case such feelings of right and wrong as then existed will have been confined to the family. But when a group of families combine and form the tribe, all those feelings of confidence, justice, etc., which were formerly characteristic of the smaller group are expanded to cover the larger one. With the expansion of the tribe to the nation we have a further development of the same phenomenon. There is no new creation, there is nothing more than expansion and development.

The process does not and cannot, obviously, stop here. From the tribe to the nation, from the nation to the collection of nations which we call an empire, and from the empire to the whole of humanity. That seems the inevitable direction of the process, and there does not require profound insight to see it already on the way. Development of national life involves a growing interdependence of the world of humankind. Of hardly any nation can it be said to-day that it is self-supporting or self-contained or independent. There is nothing national or sectarian in science, and it is to science that we have to look for our principal help. All over the world we utilize each other's discoveries and profit by each other's knowledge. Even economic interdependence carries with it the same lesson. The human environment gets gradually broader and wider, and the feelings that have hitherto been expanded over the narrower area have now to be expanded over the wider one. It is the gradual development of a human nature that is becoming adapted to a conception of mankind as an organic unit. Naturally, in the process of adaptation there is conflict between the narrower ideals, conserved in our educational influences, and the wider ones. There are still large numbers of those who, unable to picture the true nature of the evolutionary process owing to their own defective education, yet think of the world in terms of a few centuries ago, and still wave the flag of a political nationalism as though that were the end of social growth, instead of its being an early and transient expression of it. But this conflict is inevitable, and the persistence of that type can no more ensure its permanent domination than the persistence of the medicine man in the person of the existing clergyman can give permanence to the religious idea.

There is, then, no mystery about the fact of morality. It is no more of a mystery than is the compilation of the multiplication table, and it has no greater need of a supernatural sanction than has the law of gravitation. Morality is a natural fact, and its enforcement and growth are brought about by natural means. In its lower form, morality is no more than an expression of those conditions under which social life is possible, and in its higher one, an expression of those ideal conditions under which corporate life is desirable. In studying morality we are really studying the physiology of associated life, and that study aims at the determination of the conditions under which the best form of living is possible. It is thus that here, as elsewhere, man is thrown back upon himself for enlightenment and help. And if the process is a slow one we may at least console ourselves with the reflection that the labours of each generation are making the weapons which we bring to the fight keener and better able to do their work.

CHAPTER XV
MORALITY WITHOUT GOD. (*Continued.*)

In the preceding chapter I have been concerned with providing the most meagre of skeleton outlines of the way in which our moral laws and our moral sense have come into existence. To make this as clear as possible the chapter was restricted to exposition. Controversial points were avoided. And as a matter of fact there are many religionists who might concede the truth of what has been said concerning the way in which morality has arisen, and the nature of the forces that have assisted in its development. But they would proceed to argue, as men like Mr. Balfour and Mr. Benjamin Kidd, with others of the like, have argued, that a natural morality lacks all coercive power. The Freethought explanation of morality, they say, is plausible enough, and may be correct, but in conduct we have to deal not merely with the correctness of things but with sanctions and motives that exercise a compulsive influence on men and women. The religionist, it is argued, has such a compulsive force in the belief in God and in the effect on our future life of our obedience or disobedience to his commands. But what kind of coercion can a purely naturalistic system of morals exert? If a man is content to obey the naturalistic command to practise certain virtues and to abstain from certain vices, well and good. But suppose he chooses to disregard it. What then? Above all, on what compulsion is a man to disregard his own inclinations to act as seems desirable to himself, and not in conformity with the general welfare? We disregard the religious appeal as pure sentimentalism, or worse, and we at once institute an ethical sentimentalism which is, in practice, foredoomed to failure.

Or to put the same point in another way. Each individual, we say, should so act as to promote the general welfare. Freethinker and religionist are in agreement here. And so long as one's inclinations jump with the advice no difficulty presents itself. But suppose a man's inclinations do not run in the desired direction? You tell him that he must act so as to promote the general well-being, and he replies that he is not concerned with the promotion of the public welfare. You say that he *ought* to act differently, and he replies, "My happiness must consist in what I regard as such, not in other people's conception of what it should be." You proceed to point out that by persisting in his present line of conduct he is laying up trouble for the future, and he retorts, "I am willing to take the risk." What is to be done with him? Can naturalism show that in acting in that way a man is behaving unreasonably, that is, in the sense that he can be shown to be really acting against his own interests, and that if he knew better he would act differently?

Now before attempting a reply to this it is worth while pointing out that whatever strength there may be in this criticism when directed against naturalism, it is equally strong when directed against supernaturalism. We can see this at once if we merely vary the terms. You tell a man to act in this or that way "in the name of God." He replies, "I do not believe in God," and your injunction loses all force. Or, if he believes in God, and you threaten him with the pains and penalties of a future life, he may reply, "I am quite willing to risk a probable punishment hereafter for a certain pleasure here." And it is certain that many do take the risk, whether they express their determination to do so in as many words or not.

What is a supernaturalist compelled to do in this case? His method of procedure is bound to be something like the following. First of all he will seek to create assent to a particular proposition such as "God exists, and also that a belief in his existence creates an obligation to act in this or that manner in accordance with what is believed to be his will." That proposition once established, his next business will be to bring the subject's inclinations into line with a prescribed course of action. He is thus acting in precisely the same manner as is the naturalist who starts from an altogether different set of premises. And both are resting their teaching of morals upon an intellectual proposition to which assent is either implied or expressed. And that lies at the basis of all ethical teaching—not ethical practice, be it observed, but teaching. The precise form in which this intellectual proposition is cast matters little. It may be the existence of God, or it may be a particular view of human nature or of human evolution, but it is there, and in either case the authoritative character of moral precepts exists for such as accept it, and for none other. Moral practice is rooted in life, but moral theory is a different matter.

So far, then, it is clear that the complaint that Freethought ethics has nothing about it of a compulsive or authoritative character is either a begging of the question or it is absurd.

Naturalistic ethics really assert three things. The first is that the continuance of life ensures the performance of a certain level of conduct, conduct being merely one of the means by which human beings react to the necessities of their environment. Second, it asserts that a proper understanding of the conditions of existence will in the normally constituted mind strengthen the development of a feeling of obligation to act in such and such a manner; and that while all non-reasonable conduct is not immoral, all immoral conduct is fundamentally irrational. Third, there is the further assumption that at bottom individual and general welfare are not contradictory, but two aspects of the same thing.

Concerning the second point, Sir Leslie Stephen warns us (*Science of Ethics*, p. 437) that every attempt so to state the ethical principle that disobedience will be "unreasonable" is "doomed to failure in a world which is not made up of working syllogisms." And for the other two points Professor Sorley (*Ethics of Naturalism*, p. 42) tells us that "It is difficult ... to offer any consideration fitted to convince the individual that it is reasonable for him to seek the happiness of the community rather than his own"; while Mr. Benjamin Kidd asserts that "the interests of the individual and those of the social organism are not either identical or capable of being reconciled, as has been necessarily assumed in all those systems of ethics which have sought to establish a naturalistic basis of conduct. The two are fundamentally and inherently irreconcilable, and a large proportion of the existing individuals at any time have ... no personal interest whatever in the progress of the race, or in the social development we are undergoing."

It has already been said that however difficult it may be to establish the precise relationship between reason and ethical commands, such a connection must be assumed, whether we base our ethics on naturalistic or supernaturalistic considerations. And it cannot be denied by anyone to-day that a causal relation must exist between actions and their consequences, whether those causal consequences be of the natural and non-moral kind, or of the more definitely moral order such as exists in the shape of social approval and disapproval. And if we once grant that, then it seems quite allowable to assume that provided a man perceives the reason underlying moral judgments, and also the justification for the sense of approval and disapproval expressed, we have as much reason for calling his conduct reasonable or unreasonable as we have for applying the same terms to a man's behaviour in dressing in view of the variations of the temperature.

Consequently, while I agree that *in the present state of knowledge* it is impossible in all cases to demonstrate that immoral conduct is irrational in the sense that it would be unreasonable to refuse assent to a mathematical proposition, there seems no justification for regarding such a state of things as of necessity permanent. If a scientific system of ethics consists in formulating rules for the profitable guidance of life, not only does their formulation presuppose a certain constancy in the laws of human nature and of the world in general, but the assumption is also involved that one day it may be possible to give to moral laws the same precision that now is attached to physiological laws and to label departure from them as "unreasonable" in a very real sense of the word.

The other objection that it is impossible to establish a "reasonable" relation between individual and social well-being arises from a dual confusion as to what is the proper sphere of ethics, and of the mutual relation of the individual and society. To take an individual and ask, "Why should he act so as to promote the general welfare?" is to imply that ethical rules may have an application to man out of relation with his fellows. That, we have already seen, is quite wrong, since moral rules fail to be intelligible once we separate man from his fellows. Discussing ethics while leaving out social life is like discussing the functions of the lungs and leaving out of account the existence of an atmosphere.

If, then, instead of treating the individual and society as two distinct things, either of which may profit at the expense of the other, we treat them as two sides of the same thing, each an abstraction when treated alone, the problem is simplified, and the solution becomes appreciably easier. For the essential truth here is that just as there is no such thing as a society in the absence of the individuals composing it, so the individual, as we know him, disappears when we strip him of all that he is in virtue of his being a part of the social structure. Every one of the characteristic human qualities has been developed in response to the requirements of the social medium. It is in virtue of this that morality has anything of an imperative nature connected with it, for if man is, to use Sir Leslie Stephen's phrase, a cell in the social tissue, receiving injury as the body social is injured, and benefitting as it is benefitted, then the refusal of a man to act so that he may promote the general welfare can be shown to be unreasonable, and also unprofitable to the individual himself. In other words, our efficiency as an individual must be measured in terms of our fitness to form part of the social structure, and consequently the antithesis between social and personal well-being is only on the surface. Deeper knowledge and a more exact understanding reveals them as two sides of the same fact.

It may be granted to Mr. Kidd that "a large proportion of the existing individuals at any time" have no *conscious* interest in "the progress of the race or in the development we are undergoing," and that is only what one would expect, but it would be absurd to therefore come to the conclusion that no such identity of interest exists. Molière's character, who all his life had been talking prose without knowing it, is only a type of the majority of folk who all their lives are acting in accordance with principles of which they are ignorant, and which they may even repudiate when they are explained to them. From one point of view the whole object of a scientific morality is to awaken a conscious recognition of the principles underlying conduct, and by this means to strengthen the disposition to right action. We make explicit in language what has hitherto been implicit in action, and thus bring conscious effort to the aid of non-conscious or semi-conscious behaviour.

In the light of the above consideration the long and wordy contest that has been waged between "Altruists" and "Egoists" is seen to be very largely a waste of time and a splutter of words. If it can be shown on the one hand that all men are not animated by the desire to benefit self, it is as easy to demonstrate that so long as human nature is human nature, all conduct must be an expression of individual character, and that even the morality of self-sacrifice is self-regarding viewed from the personal feelings of the agent. And it being clear that the position of Egoist and Altruist, while each expressing a truth, is neither expressing the whole truth, and that each does in fact embody a definite error, it seems probable that here, as in so many other cases, the truth lies between the two extremes, and that a reconciliation may be effected along these lines.

Taking animal life as a whole it is at least clear that what are called the self-regarding feelings must come first in order of development. Even with the lower races of human beings there is less concern shown with the feelings and welfare of others than is the case with the higher races of men. Or, again, with children we have these feelings strongest in childhood and undergoing a gradual expansion as maturity is reached. This is brought about, as was shown in the last chapter, not by the destruction of existing feelings, but by their extension to an ever widening area. There is a transformation, or an elaboration of existing feelings under the pressure of social growth. One may say that ethical development does not proceed by the destruction of the feeling of self-interest, so much as by its extension to a wider field. Ethical growth is thus on all fours with biological growth. In biology we are all familiar with the truth that maintenance of life is dependent upon the existence of harmonious relations between an organism and its environment. Yet it is not always recognized that this principle is as true of the moral self as it is of the physical structure, nor that in human evolution the existence of others becomes of increasing importance and significance. For not only do I have to adapt myself, mentally and morally, to the society now existing, but also to societies that have long since passed away and have left their contribution to the building up of *my* environment in the shape of institutions and beliefs and literature.

We have in this one more illustration that while the environment of the animal is overwhelmingly physical in character, that of man tends to become overwhelmingly social or psychological. Desires are created that can only be gratified by the presence and the labour of others. Feelings arise that have direct reference to others, and in numerous ways a body of "altruistic" feeling is created. So by social growth first, and afterwards by reflection, man is taught that the only life that is enjoyable to himself is one that is lived in the companionship and by the co-operation of others. As Professor Ziegler well puts the process:—

> Not only on the one hand does it concern the interests of the general welfare that every individual should take care of himself outwardly and inwardly; maintain his health; cultivate his faculties and powers; sustain his position, honour, and worth, and so his own welfare being secured, diffuse around him happiness and comfort; but also, on the other hand, it concerns the personal, well understood interests of the individual himself that he should promote the interests of others, contribute to their happiness, serve their interests, and even make sacrifices for them. Just as one forgoes a momentary pleasure in order to secure a lasting and greater enjoyment, so the individual willingly sacrifices his personal welfare and comfort for the sake of society in order to share in the welfare of this society; he buries his individual well-being in order that he may see it rise in richer and fuller abundance in the welfare and happiness of the whole community (*Social Ethics*, pp. 59-60).

These motives are not of necessity conscious ones. No one imagines that before performing a social action each one sits down and goes through a more or less elaborate calculation. All that has been written on this head concerning a "Utilitarian calculus" is poor fun and quite beside the mark. In this matter, as in so many others, it is the evolutionary process which demands consideration, and generations of social struggle, by weeding out individuals whose inclinations were of a pronounced anti-social kind, and tribes in which the cohesion between its members was weak, have resulted in bringing about more or less of an identification between individual desires and the general welfare. It is not a question of conscious evolution so much as of our becoming conscious of an evolution that is taking place, and in discussing the nature of morals one is bound to go beyond the expressed reasons for conduct—more often wrong than right—and discover the deeper and truer causes of instincts and actions. When this is done it will be found that while it is absolutely impossible to destroy the connection between conduct and self-regarding actions, there is proceeding a growing identity between the gratification of desire and the well-being of the whole. This will be, not because of some fantastical or ascetic teaching of self-sacrifice, but because man being an expression of social life is bound to find in activities that have a social reference the beginning and end of his conduct.

The fears of a morality without God are, therefore, quite unfounded. If what has been said be granted, it follows that all ethical rules are primarily on the same level as a generalization in any of the sciences. Just as the "laws" of astronomy or of biology reduce to order the apparently chaotic phenomena of their respective departments, so ethical laws seek to reduce to an intelligible order the conditions of individual and social betterment. There can be no ultimate antithesis between individual reason and the highest form of social conduct, although there may exist an apparent conflict between the two, chiefly owing to the fact that we are often unable to trace the remote effects of conduct on self and society. Nor can there be an ultimate or permanent conflict between the true interests of the individual and of society at large. That such an opposition does exist in the minds of many is true, but it is here worthy of note that the clearest and most profound thinkers have always found in the field of social effort the best sphere for the gratification of their desires. And here again we may confidently hope that an increased and more accurate appreciation of the causes that determine human welfare will do much to diminish this antagonism. At any rate it is clear that human nature has been moulded in accordance with the reactions of self and society in such a way that even the self has become an expression of social life, and with this dual aspect before us there is no reason why emphasis should be laid on one factor rather than on the other.

To sum up. Eliminating the form of coercion that is represented by a policeman, earthly or otherwise, we may safely say that a naturalistic ethics has all the coercive force that can be possessed by any system. And it has this advantage over the coercive force of the supernaturalist, that while the latter tends to weaken with the advance of intelligence, the former gains strength as men and women begin to more clearly appreciate the true conditions of social life and development. It is in this way that there is finally established a connection between what is "reasonable" and what is right. In this case it is the function of reason to discover the forces that have made for the moralization—really the socialization—of man, and so strengthen man's moral nature by demonstrating the fundamental identity between his own welfare and that of the group to which he belongs. That the coercion may in some cases be quite ineffective must be admitted. There will always, one fancies, be cases where the personal character refuses to adapt itself to the current social state. That is a form of mal-adaptation which society will always have to face, exactly as it has to face cases of atavism in other directions. But the socializing and moralizing process continues. And however much this may be, in its earlier stages, entangled with conceptions of the supernatural, it is certain that growth will involve the disappearance of that factor here as it has done elsewhere.

CHAPTER XVI
CHRISTIANITY AND MORALITY

The association of religion with morality is a very ancient one. This is not because the one is impossible without the other, we have already shown that this is not the case. The reason is that unless religious beliefs are associated with certain essential social activities their continuance is almost impossible. Thus it happens in the course of social evolution that just in proportion as man learns to rely upon the purely social activities to that extent religion is driven to dwell more upon them and to claim kinship with them.

While this is true of religions in general, it applies with peculiar force to Christianity. And in the last two or three centuries we have seen the emphasis gradually shifted from a set of doctrines, upon the acceptance of which man's eternal salvation depends, to a number of ethical and social teachings with which Christianity, as such, has no vital concern. The present generation of Christian believers has had what is called the moral aspect of Christianity so constantly impressed upon them, and the essential and doctrinal aspect so slurred over, that many of them have come to accept the moral teaching associated with Christianity as its most important aspect. More than that, they have come to regard the immense superiority of Christianity as one of those statements the truth of which can be doubted by none but the most obtuse. To have this alleged superiority of Christian ethical teaching questioned appears to them proof of some lack of moral development on the part of the questioner.

To this type of believer it will come with something of a shock to be told quite plainly and without either circumlocution or apology that his religion is of an intensely selfish and egoistic character, and that its ethical influence is of a kind that is far from admirable. It will shock him because he has for so long been told that his religion is the very quintessence of unselfishness, he has for so long been telling it to others, and he has been able for so many generations to make it uncomfortable for all those who took an opposite view, that he has camouflaged both the nature of his own motives and the tendency of his religion.

From one point of view this is part of the general scheme in virtue of which the Christian Church has given currency to the legend that the doctrines taught by it represented a tremendous advance in the development of the race. In sober truth it represented nothing of the kind. That the elements of Christian religious teaching existed long before Christianity as a religious system was known to the world is now a commonplace with all students of comparative religions, and is admitted by most Christian writers of repute. Even in form the Christian doctrines represented but a small advance upon their pagan prototypes, but it is only when one bears in mind the fact that the best minds of antiquity were rapidly throwing off these superstitions and leading the world to a more enlightened view of things, we realize that in the main Christianity represented a step backward in the intellectual evolution of the race. What we then see is Christianity reaffirming and re-establishing most of the old superstitions in forms in which only the more ignorant classes of antiquity accepted them. We have an assertion of demonism in its crudest forms, an affirmation of the miraculous that the educated in the Roman world had learned to laugh at, and which is to-day found among the savage people of the earth, while every form of scientific thought was looked upon as an act of impiety. The scientific eclipse that overtook the old pagan civilization was one of the inevitable consequences of the triumph of Christianity. From the point of view of general culture the retrogressive nature of Christianity is unmistakable. It has yet to be recognized that the same statement holds good in relation even to religion. One day the world will appreciate the fact that no greater disaster ever overtook the world than the triumph of the Christian Church.

For the moment, however, we are only concerned with the relation of Christianity to morality. And here my thesis is that Christianity is an essentially selfish creed masking its egoistic impulses under a cover of unselfishness and self-sacrifice. To that it will probably be said that the charge breaks down on the fact that Christian teaching is full of the exhortation that this world is of no moment, that we gain salvation by learning to ignore its temptations and to forgo its pleasures, and that it is, above all other faiths, the religion of personal sacrifice. And that this teaching is there it would be stupid to deny. But this does not disprove what has been said, indeed, analysis only serves to make the truth still plainer. That many Christians have given up the prizes of the world is too plain to be denied; that they have forsaken all that many struggle to possess is also plain. But when this has been admitted there still remains the truth that there is a vital distinction in the consideration of whether a man gives up the world in order to save his own soul, or whether he saves his soul as a consequence of losing the world. In this matter it is the aim that is important, not only to the outsider who may be passing judgment, but more importantly to the agent himself. It is the effect of the motive on character with its subsequent flowering in social life that must be considered.

The first count in the indictment here is that the Christian appeal is essentially a selfish one. The aim is not the saving of others but of one's self. If other people must be saved it is because their salvation is believed to be essential to the saving of one's own soul. That this involves, or may involve, a surrender of one's worldly possessions or comfort, is of no moment. Men will forgo many pleasures and give up much when they have what they believe to be a greater purpose in view. We see this in directions quite unconnected with religion. Politics will show us examples of men who have forsaken many of what are to others the comforts of life in the hopes of gaining power and fame. Others will deny themselves many pleasures in the prospect of achieving some end which to them is of far greater value than the things they are renouncing. And it is the same principle that operates in the case of religious devotees. There is no reason to doubt but that when a young woman forsakes the world and goes into a cloister she is surrendering much that has considerable attractions for her. But what she gives is to her of small importance to what she gains in return. And if one believed in Christianity, in immortal damnation, with the intensity of the great Christian types of character, it would be foolish not to surrender things of so little value for others of so great and transcendent importance.

To do Christians justice they have not usually made a secret of their aim. Right through Christian literature there runs the teaching that it is the desire of personal and immortal salvation that inspires them, and they have affirmed over and over again that but for the prospect of being paid back with tremendous interest in the next world they could see no reason for being good in this one. That is emphatically the teaching of the New Testament and of the greatest of Christian characters. You are to give in secret that you may be rewarded openly, to cast your bread upon the waters that it may be returned to you, and Paul's counsel is that if there be no resurrection from the dead then we may eat, drink, and be merry for death only is before us. Thus, what you do is in the nature of a deliberate and conscious investment on which you will receive a handsome dividend in the next world. And your readiness to invest will be exactly proportionate to your conviction of the soundness of the security. But there is in all this no perception of the truly ethical basis of conduct, no indication of the inevitable consequences of conduct on character. What is good is determined by what it is believed will save one's own soul and increase the dividend in the next world. What is bad is anything that will imperil the security. It is essentially an appeal to what is grasping and selfish in human nature, and while you may hide the true character of a thing by the lavish use of attractive phrases, you cannot hinder it working out its consequences in actual life. And the consequence of this has been that while Christian teaching has been lavish in the use of attractive phrases its actual result has been to create a type of character that has been not so much immoral as *amoral*. And with that type the good that has been done on the one side has been more than counterbalanced by the evil done on the other.

What the typical Christian character had in mind in all that he did was neither the removal of suffering nor of injustice, but the salvation of his own soul. That justified everything so long as it was believed to contribute to that end. The social consequences of what was done simply did not count. And if, instead of taking mere phrases from the principal Christian writers, we carefully examine their meaning we shall see that they were strangely devoid of what is now understood by the expression "moral incentive." The more impressive the outbreak of Christian piety the clearer does this become. No one could have illustrated the Christian ideal of self-sacrifice better than did the saints and monks of the earlier Christian centuries. Such a character as the famous St. Simon Stylites, living for years on his pillar, filthy and verminous, and yet the admired of Christendom, with the lives of numerous other saints, whose sole claim to be remembered is that they lived the lives of worse than animals in the selfish endeavours to save their shrunken souls, will well illustrate this point. If it entered the diseased imagination of these men that the road to salvation lay through attending to the sick and the needy, they were quite ready to labour in that direction; but of any desire to remove the horrible social conditions that prevailed, or to remedy the injustice of which their clients were the victims, there is seldom a trace. And, on the other hand, if they believed that their salvation involved getting away from human society altogether and leading the life of a hermit, they were as ready to do that. If it meant the forsaking of husband or wife or parent or child, these were left without compunction, and their desertion was counted as proof of righteousness. The lives of the saints are full of illustrations of this. Professor William James well remarks, in his *Varieties of Religious Experience*, that "In gentle characters, where devoutness is intense and the intellect feeble, we have an imaginative absorption in the love of God to the exclusion of all practical human interests.... When the love of God takes possession of such a mind it expels all human loves and human uses." Of the Blessed St. Mary Alacoque, her biographer points out that as she became absorbed in the love of Christ she became increasingly useless to the practical life of the convent. Of St. Teresa, James remarks that although a woman of strong intellect his impression of her was a feeling of pity that so much vitality of soul should have found such poor employment.

And of so famous a character as St. Augustine a Christian writer, Mr. A. C. Benson, remarks:—

> I was much interested in reading St. Augustine's *Confessions* lately to recognize how small a part, after his conversion, any aspirations for the welfare of humanity seem to play in his mind compared with the consciousness of his own personal relations with God. It was this which gave him his exuberant sense of joy and peace, and his impulse was rather the impulse of sharing a wonderful and beautiful secret with others than an immediate desire for their welfare, forced out of him, so to speak, by his own exultation rather than drawn out of him by compassion for the needs of others.

That is one of the most constant features which emerges from a careful study of the character of Christian types. St. Francis commenced his career by leaving his parents. John Fox did the same. In that Puritan classic, *The Pilgrim's Progress*, one of the outstanding features is the striking absence of emphasis on the value of the social and domestic virtues, and the Rev. Principal Donaldson notes this as one of the features of early Christian literature in general. Christian preaching was for centuries full of contemptuous references to "filthy rags of righteousness," "mere morality," etc. The aim of the saints was a purely selfish and personal one. It was not even a refined or a metaphysical selfishness. It was a simple teaching that the one thing essential was to save one's own soul, and that the main reason for doing good in this world was to reap a benefit from it in the world to come. If it can properly be called morality, it was conduct placed out at the highest rate of interest. Christianity may often have used a naturally lofty character, it was next to impossible for it to create one.

If one examines the attack made by Christians upon Freethought morality, it is surprising how often the truth of what has been said is implied. For the complaint here is, in the main, not that naturalism fails to give an adequate account of the nature and development of morality, but that it will not satisfy mankind, and so fails to act as an adequate motive to right conduct. When we enquire precisely what is meant by this, we learn that if there is no belief in God, and if there is no expectation of a future state in which rewards and punishments will be dispensed, there remains no inducement to the average man or woman to do right. It is the moral teaching of St. Paul over again. We are in the region of morality as a deliberate investment, and we have the threat that if the interest is not high enough or certain enough to satisfy the dividend hunting appetite of the true believer, then the investment will be withdrawn. Really this is a complaint, not that the morality which ignores Christianity is too low but that it is too high. It is doubted whether human nature, particularly Christian human nature, can rise to such a level, and whether, unless you can guarantee a Christian a suitable reward for not starving his family or for not robbing his neighbour, he will continue to place any value on decency or honesty.

So to state the case makes the absurdity of the argument apparent, but unless that is what is meant it is difficult to make it intelligible. To reply that Christians do not require these inducements to behave with a tolerable amount of decency is not a statement that I should dispute; on the contrary, I would affirm it. It is the Christian defender who makes himself and his fellow believers worse than the Freethinker believes them to be. For it is part of the case of the Freethinker that the morality of the Christian has really no connection with his religion, and that the net influence of his creed is to confuse and distort his moral sense instead of developing it. It is the argument of the Christian that makes the Freethinker superior to the Christian; it is the Freethinker who declines the compliment and who asserts that the social forces are adequate to guarantee the continuance of morality in the complete absence of religious belief.

How little the Christian religion appreciates the nature of morality is seen by the favourite expression of Christian apologists that the tendency of non-religion is to remove all moral "restraints." The use of the word is illuminating. To the Christian morality is no more than a system of restraints which aim at preventing a man gratifying his appetite in certain directions. It forbids him certain enjoyments here, and promises him as a reward for his abstention a greater benefit hereafter. And on that assumption he argues, quite naturally, that if there be no after life then there seems no reason why man should undergo the "restraints" which moral rules impose. On this scheme man is a born criminal and God an almighty policeman. That is the sum of orthodox Christian morality. To assume that this conception of conduct can have a really elevating effect on life is to misunderstand the nature of the whole of the ethical and social problem.

What has been said may go some distance towards suggesting an answer to the question so often asked as to the reason for the moral failure of Christianity. For that it has been a moral failure no one can doubt. Nay, it is an assertion made very generally by Christians themselves. Right from New Testament times the complaint that the conduct of believers has fallen far short of what it should have been is constantly met with. And there is not a single direction in which Christians can claim a moral superiority over other and non-Christian peoples. They are neither kinder, more tolerant, more sober, more chaste, nor more truthful than are non-Christian people. Nor is it quite without significance that those nations that pride themselves most upon their Christianity are what they are. Their state reflects the ethical spirit I have been trying to describe. For when we wipe out the disguising phrases which we use to deceive ourselves—and it is almost impossible to continually deceive others unless we do manage to deceive ourselves—when we put on one side the "rationalizing" phrases about Imperial races, carrying civilization to the dark places of the earth, bearing the white man's burden, peopling the waste places of the earth, etc., we may well ask what for centuries have the Christian nations of the world been but so many gangs of freebooters engaged in world-wide piracy? All over the world they have gone, fighting, stealing, killing, lying, annexing, in a steadily rising crescendo. To be possessed of natural wealth, without the means of resisting aggression, has for four centuries been to invite the depredations of some one or more of the Christian powers. It is the Christian powers that have militarized the world in the name of the Prince of Peace, and made piracy a national occupation in the name of civilization. Everywhere they have done these things under the shelter of their religion and with the sanction of their creed. Christianity has offered no effective check to the cupidity of man, its chief work has been to find an outlet for it in a disguised form. To borrow a term from the psycho-analysts, the task of Christianity has been to "rationalize" certain ugly impulses, and so provide the opportunity for their continuous expression. The world of to-day is beginning to recognize the intellectual weakness of Christianity; what it has next to learn is that its moral bankruptcy is no less assured.

One of the great obstacles in the way of this is the sentimentalism of many who have given up all intellectual adherence to the Christian creed. The power of the Christian Church has been so great, it has for so long had control of the machinery of public education and information, that many find it almost impossible to conclude that the ethical spirit of Christianity is as alien to real progress as are its cosmical teachings. The very hugeness of this century-old imposture blinds many to its inherent defects. And yet the continuous and world-wide moral failure of Christianity can only be accounted for on the ground that it had a fatal moral defect from the start. I have suggested above what is the nature of that defect. It has never regarded morality as a natural social growth, but only as something imposed upon man from without. It has had no other reason for its existence than the fear of punishment and the hope of reward. Christian morality is the morality of the stock exchange *plus* the intellectual outlook of the savage. And with that in control of national destinies our surprise should be, not that things are as they are, but rather that with so great a handicap the world has contrived to reach its present moderate degree of development.

CHAPTER XVII
RELIGION AND PERSECUTION

Intolerance is one of the most general of what we may call the mental vices. It is so general that few people seem to look upon it as a fault, and not a few are prepared to defend it as a virtue. When it assumes an extreme form, and its consequences are unpleasantly obvious, it may meet with condemnation, but usually its nature is disguised under a show of earnestness and sincere conviction. And, indeed, no one need feel called upon to dispute the sincerity and the earnestness of the bigot. As we have already pointed out, that may easily be seen and admitted. All that one need remark is that sincerity is no guarantee of accuracy, and earnestness naturally goes with a conviction strongly held, whether the conviction be grounded on fact or fancy. The essential question is not whether a man holds an opinion strongly, but whether he has taken sufficient trouble to say that he has a right to have that opinion. Has he taken the trouble to acquaint himself with the facts upon which the expressed opinion is professedly based? Has he made a due allowance for possible error, and for the possibility of others seeing the matter from another and a different point of view? If these questions were frankly and truthfully answered, it would be found that what we have to face in the world is not so much opinion as prejudice.

Some advance in human affairs is indicated when it is found necessary to apologise for persecution, and a still greater one when men and women feel ashamed of it. It is some of these apologies at which we have now to glance, and also to determine, if possible, the probable causes of the change in opinion that has occurred in relation to the subject of persecution.

A favourite argument with the modern religionist is that the element of persecution, which it is admitted, has hitherto been found in association with religion, is not due to religion as such, but results from its connection with the secular power. Often, it is argued, the State for its own purposes has seen fit to ally itself with the Church, and when that has taken place the representatives of the favoured Church have not been strong enough to withstand the temptation to use physical force in the maintenance of their position. Hence the generalization that a State Church is always a persecuting Church, with the corollary that a Church, as such, has nothing to do with so secular a thing as persecution.

The generalization has all the attractiveness which appeals to those who are not in the habit of looking beneath the surface, and in particular to those whose minds are still in thraldom to religious beliefs. It is quite true that State Churches have always persecuted, and it is equally true that persecution on a general scale could not have been carried on without the assistance of the State. On the other hand, it is just as true that all Churches have persecuted within the limits of their opportunity. There is no exception to this rule in any age or country. On a wider survey it is also clear that all forms of religious belief carry with them a tendency to persecution more or less marked. A close examination of the facts will show that it is the tendency to toleration that is developed by the secular power, and the opposite tendency manifested by religion.

It is also argued that intolerance is not a special quality of religion; it is rather a fault of human nature. There is more truth in this than in the previous plea, but it slurs over the indictment rather than meets it. At any rate, it is the same human nature that meets us in religion that fronts us in other matters, and there is no mistaking the fact that intolerance is far more pronounced in relation to religion than to any other subject. In secular matters—politics, science, literature, or art—opinions may differ, feelings run high, and a degree of intolerance be exhibited, but the right to differ remains unquestioned. Moreover, the settlement of opinion by discussion is recognized. In religion it is the very right of difference that is challenged, it is the right of discussion that is denied. And it is in connection with religion alone that intolerance is raised to the level of a virtue. Refusal to discuss the validity of a religious opinion will be taken as the sign of a highly developed spiritual nature, and a tolerance of diverging opinions as an indication of unbelief. If a political leader refused to stand upon the same platform with political opponents, on non-political questions, nearly everyone would say that such conduct was intolerable. But how many religious people are there who would see anything wrong in the Archbishop of Canterbury refusing to stand upon the same platform as a well-known Atheist?

We are here approaching the very heart of the subject, and in what follows I hope to make clear the truth of the following propositions: (1) That the great culture ground of intolerance is religion; (2) That the natural tendency of secular affairs is to breed tolerance; (3) That the alliance of religion with the State has fostered persecution by the State, the restraining influences coming from the secular half of the partnership; (4) That the decline of persecution is due to causes that are quite unconnected with religious beliefs.

The first three points can really be taken together. So far as can be seen there is no disinclination among primitive peoples to discuss the pros and cons of matters that are unconnected with religious beliefs. So soon as we get people at a culture stage where the course of events is seen to be decided by human action, there goes on a tolerance of conflicting opinions that is in striking contrast with what occurs with such matters as are believed to directly involve the action of deity. One could not expect things to be otherwise. In the carrying on of warfare, as with many other tribal activities, so many of the circumstances are of a determinable character, and are clearly to be settled by an appeal to judgment and experience, that very early in social history they must have presented themselves as a legitimate field for discussion, and to discussion, as Bagehot says, nothing is sacred. And as a matter of fact we have a survival of this to-day. However intolerant the character, so long as we are dealing with secular matters it is admitted that differences of opinion must be tolerated, and are, indeed, necessary if we are to arrive at the wisest conclusion. The most autocratic of monarchs will call upon his advisers and take their dissension from his own views as a matter of course. But when we get to the field of religion, it is no longer a question of the legitimacy of difference, but of its wrongness. For a religious man to admit a discussion as to whether his religious belief is founded on fact or not is to imply a doubt, and no thoroughly religious man ever encourages that. What we have is prayers to be saved from doubt, and deliberate efforts to keep away from such conditions and circumstances as may suggest the possibility of wrong. The ideal religious character is the one who never doubts.

It may also be noted, in passing, that in connection with religion there is nothing to check intolerance at any stage. In relation to secular matters an opinion is avowedly based upon verifiable facts and has no value apart from those facts. The facts are common property, open to all, and may be examined by all. In religion facts of a common and verifiable kind are almost wanting. The facts of the religious life are mainly of an esoteric character — visions, intuitions, etc. And while on the secular side discussion is justified because of the agreement which results from it, on the religious side the value of discussion is discounted because it never does lead to agreement. The more people discuss religion the more pronounced the disagreement. That is one reason why the world over the only method by which people have been brought to a state of agreement in religious doctrines is by excluding all who disagreed. It is harmony in isolation.

Now if we turn to religion we can see that from the very beginning the whole tendency here was to stifle difference of opinion, and so establish intolerance as a religious duty. The Biblical story of Jonah is a case that well illustrates the point. God was not angry with the rest of the ship's inhabitants, it was Jonah only who had given offence. But to punish Jonah a storm was sent and the whole crew was in danger of shipwreck. In their own defence the sailors were driven to throw Jonah overboard. Jonah's disobedience was not, therefore, his concern alone. All with him were involved; God was ready to punish the whole for the offence of one.

Now if for the ship we take a primitive tribe, and for Jonah a primitive heretic, or one who for some reason or other has omitted a service to the gods, we have an exact picture of what actually takes place. In primitive societies rights are not so much individual as they are social. Every member of the tribe is responsible to the members of other tribes for any injury that may have been done. And as with the members of another tribe, so with the relation of the tribe to the gods. If an individual offends them the whole of the tribe may suffer. There is a splendid impartiality about the whole arrangement, although it lacks all that we moderns understand by Justice. But the point here is that it makes the heretic not merely a mistaken person, but a dangerous character. His heresy involves treason to the tribe, and in its own defence it is felt that the heretic must be suppressed. How this feeling lingers in relation to religion is well seen in the fact that there are still with us large numbers of very pious people who are ready to see in a bad harvest, a war, or an epidemic, a judgment of God on the whole of the people for the sins of a few. It is this element that has always given to religious persecutions the air of a solemn duty. To suppress the heretic is something that is done in the interests of the whole of the people. Persecution becomes both a religious and a social duty.

The pedigree of religious persecution is thus clear. It is inherent in religious belief, and to whatever extent human nature is prone to intolerance, the tendency has been fostered and raised to the status of a virtue by religious teaching and practice. Religion has served to confuse man's sense of right here as elsewhere.

We have thus two currents at work. On the one hand, there is the influence of the secular side of life, which makes normally for a greater tolerance of opinion, on the other side there is religion which can only tolerate a difference of opinion to the extent that religious doctrines assume a position of comparative unimportance. Instead of it being the case that the Church has been encouraged to persecute by the State, the truth is the other way about. I know all that may be said as to the persecutions that have been set on foot by vested interests and by governments, but putting on one side the consideration that this begs the question of how far it has been the consequence of the early influence of religion, there are obvious limits beyond which a secular persecution cannot go. A government cannot destroy its subjects, or if it does the government itself disappears. And the most thorough scheme of exploitation must leave its victims enough on which to live. There are numerous considerations which weigh with a secular government and which have little weight with a Church.

It may safely be said, for example, that no government in the world, in the absence of religious considerations would have committed the suicidal act which drove the Moors and the Jews from Spain.[24] As a matter of fact, the landed aristocracy of Spain resisted suggestions for expulsions for nearly a century because of the financial ruin they saw would follow. It was the driving power of religious belief that finally brought about the expulsion. Religion alone could preach that it was better for the monarch to reign over a wilderness than over a nation of Jews and unbelievers. The same thing was repeated a century later in the case of the expulsion of the Huguenots from France. Here again the crown resisted the suggestions of the Church, and for the same reason. And it is significant that when governments have desired to persecute in their own interests they have nearly always found it advantageous to do so under the guise of religion. So far, and in these instances, it may be true that the State has used religion for its own purpose of persecution, but this does not touch the important fact that, given the sanction of religion, intolerance and persecution assume the status of virtues. And to the credit of the State it must be pointed out that it has over and over again had to exert a restraining influence in the quarrels of sects. It will be questioned by few that if the regulative influence of the State had not been exerted the quarrels of the sects would have made a settled and orderly life next to impossible.

So far as Christianity is concerned it would puzzle the most zealous of its defenders to indicate a single direction in which it did anything to encourage the slightest modification of the spirit of intolerance. Mohammedans can at least point to a time when, while their religion was dominant, a considerable amount of religious freedom was allowed to those living under its control. In the palmy days of the Mohammedan rule in Spain both Jews and Christians were allowed to practise their religion with only trifling inconveniences, certainly without being exposed to the fiendish punishments that characterized Christianity all over the world. Moreover, it must never be overlooked that in Europe all laws against heresy are of Christian origin. In the old Roman Empire liberty of worship was universal. So long as the State religion was treated with a moderate amount of respect one might worship whatever god one pleased, and the number was sufficient to provide for the most varied tastes. When Christians were proceeded against it was under laws that did not aim primarily to shackle liberty of worship or of opinion. The procedure was in every case formal, the trial public, time was given for the preparation of the defence, and many of the judges showed their dislike to the prosecutions.[25] But with the Christians, instead of persecution being spasmodic it was persistent. It was not taken up by the authorities with reluctance, but with eagerness, and it was counted as the most sacred of duties. Nor was it directed against a sectarian movement that threatened the welfare of the State. The worst periods of Christian persecution were those when the State had the least to fear from internal dissension. The persecuted were not those who were guilty of neglect of social duty. On the contrary they were serving the State by the encouragement of literature, science, philosophy, and commerce. One of the Pagan Emperors, the great Trajan, had advised the magistrates not to search for Christians, and to treat anonymous accusations with contempt. Christians carried the search for heresy into a man's own household. It used the child to obtain evidence against its own parents, the wife to secure evidence against the husband; it tortured to provide dictated confessions, and placed boxes at church doors to receive anonymous accusations. It established an index of forbidden books, an institution absolutely unknown to the pagan world. The Roman trial was open, the accused could hear the charge and cite witnesses for the defence. The Christian trial was in secret; special forms were used and no witnesses for the defence were permitted. Persecution was raised to a fine art. Under Christian auspices it assumed the most damnable form known in the history of the world. "There are no wild beasts so ferocious as Christians" was the amazed comment of the Pagans on the behaviour of Christians towards each other, and the subsequent history of Christianity showed that the Pagans were but amateurs in the art of punishing for a difference of opinion.

Up to a comparatively recent time there existed a practically unanimous opinion among Christians as to the desirability of forcibly suppressing heretical opinions. Whatever the fortunes of Christianity, and whatever the differences of opinion that gradually developed among Christians there was complete unanimity on this point. Whatever changes the Protestant Reformation effected it left this matter untouched. In his *History of Rationalism* Lecky has brought forward a mass of evidence in support of this, and I must refer to that work readers who are not already acquainted with the details. Luther, in the very act of pleading for toleration, excepted "such as deny the common principles of the Christian religion, and advised that the Jews should be confined as madmen, their synagogues burned and their books destroyed." The intolerance of Calvin has became a byword; his very apology for the burning of Servetus, entitled *A Defence of the Orthodox Faith*, bore upon its title page the significant sentence "In which it is proved that heretics may justly be coerced with the sword." His follower, Knox, was only carrying out the teaching of the master in declaring that "provoking the people to idolatry ought not to be exempt from the penalty of death," and that "magistrates and people are bound to do so (inflict the death penalty) unless they will provoke the wrath of God against themselves." In every Protestant country laws against heresy were enacted. In Switzerland, Geneva, Sweden, England, Germany, Scotland, nowhere could one differ from the established faith without running the risk of torture and death. Even in America, with the exception of Maryland,[26] the same state of things prevailed. In some States Catholic priests were subject to imprisonment for life, Quaker women were whipped through the streets at the cart's tail, old men of the same denomination were pressed to death between stones. At a later date (about 1770) laws against heresy were general. "Anyone," says Fiske, —

> who should dare to speculate too freely about the nature of Christ, or the philosophy of the plan of salvation, or to express a doubt as to the plenary inspiration of every word between the two covers of the Bible, was subject to fine and imprisonment. The tithing man still arrested the Sabbath-breakers, and shut them up in the town cage in the market-place; he stopped all unnecessary riding or driving on Sunday, and haled people off to the meeting-house whether they would or no.[27]

And we have to remember that the intolerance shown in America was manifested by men who had left their own country on the ostensible ground of freedom of conscience. As a matter of fact, in Christian society genuine freedom of conscience was practically unknown. What was meant by the expression was the right to express one's own religious opinions, with the privilege of oppressing all with whom one happened to disagree. The majority of Christians would have as indignantly repudiated the assertion that they desired to tolerate non-Christian or anti-Christian opinions as they would the charge of themselves holding Atheistic ones.

How deeply ingrained was the principle that the established religion was justified in suppressing all others may be seen from a reading of such works as Locke's *Letters on Toleration*, and Milton's *Areopagitica*, which stand in the forefront of the world's writings in favour of liberty of thought and speech. Yet Locke was of opinion that "Those are not at all to be tolerated who deny the being of a God. Promises, covenants, and oaths, which are the bonds of human society, can have no hold upon an Atheist. The taking away of God, though but even in thought, dissolves all." And Milton, while holding that it was more prudent and wholesome that many be tolerated rather than all compelled, yet hastened to add "I mean not tolerated popery and open superstition, which as it extirpates all religious and civil supremacies so should itself be extirpated." In short, intolerance had become so established a part of a society saturated in religion that not even the most liberal could conceive a state of being in which all opinions should be placed upon an equal footing.

Yet a change was all the time taking place in men's opinions on this matter, a change which has in recent years culminated in the affirmation of the principle that the coercion of opinion is of all things the least desirable and the least beneficial to society at large. And as in so many other cases, it was not the gradual maturing of that principle that attracted attention so much as its statement in something like a complete and logical form. The tracing of the conditions which have led to this tremendous revolution in public opinion will complete our survey of the subject.

It has already been pointed out that in primitive societies a very important fact is that the relation of the individual to the community is of a different nature from that which exists in a later stage of culture. The whole is responsible for the part in a very literal sense, and especially so in regard to religious beliefs. Individual rights and responsibilities have but a precarious existence at best. The individual exists far more for the benefit of the tribe than the tribe can be said to exist for the benefit of the individual. The sense of corporate responsibility is strong, and even in secular affairs we see this constantly manifested. When a member of one tribe inflicts an injury upon a member of another tribe, retaliation on any one of the group to which the offending person belongs will suffice. We see the remnants of this primitive view of life in the feuds of schoolboys, and it is also manifested in the relations of nations, which move upon a lower ethical level than do individuals. Most wars are ostensibly waged because in some obscure way the nation is held responsible for the offences of one or more individuals. And an instance of the same feeling is seen in the now obsolete practice of punishing the members of a man's family when the parents happen to have committed certain offences.

In religion, as we have already pointed out, the sense of corporate responsibility completely governs primitive man's sense of his relation to the tribal gods. In the development of the tribal chief into the tribal god the ghost is credited with much the same powers as the man, with the added terror of having more subtle and terrible ways of inflicting punishment. The man who offends the ghost or the god is a standing danger to the whole of the tribe. The whole of the tribe becomes responsible for the offence committed, and the tribe in self protection must not alone take measures to punish the offender, but must also guard itself against even the possibility of the offence being perpetrated. The consequence is that there is not a religion in which one can fail to trace the presence of this primitive conception of personal and social responsibility, and consequently, where we cannot find persecution, more or less severe, and also more or less organized, in the interest of what is believed to be social welfare. In the case of the failure of the Spanish Armada to effect the conquest of England, the Spanish monarch was convinced that its non-success was partly due to his not having weeded out the heretics from his own dominion before troubling about the heretics abroad. And right down to our own day there has not been a national calamity the cause of which has not been found by numbers of religious people to lie in the fact that some members of the suffering nation have offended God. The heretic becomes, as we have already said, a social danger of the gravest description. Society must be guarded against his presence just as we learn to-day to protect ourselves against the presence of a death-dealing germ. The suppression of heresy thus becomes a social duty, because it protects society from the anger of the gods. The destruction of the heretic is substantially an act of social sanitation. Given the primitive conception of religion, affiliated to the existing conception of corporate responsibility, and persecution becomes one of the most important of social duties.

This, I believe, is not alone the root of persecution, but it serves to explain as nothing else can its persistence in social life and the fact of its having became almost a general mental characteristic. To realize this one need only bear in mind the overpowering part played by religious conceptions in early communities. There is nothing done that is not more or less under the assumed control of supernatural agencies. Fear is the dominant emotion in relation to the gods, and experience daily proves that there is nothing that can make men so brutal and so callous to the sufferings of others as can religious belief. And while there has all along been a growing liberation of the mind from the control of religion, the process has been so slow that this particular product of religious rule has had time to root itself very deeply in human nature. And it is in accordance with all that we know of the order of development that the special qualities engendered by a particular set of conditions should persist long after the conditions themselves have passed away.

The conditions that co-operate in the final breaking down of the conviction of the morality of persecution are many and various. Primarily, there is the change from the social state in which the conception of corporate responsibility is dominant to one in which there is a more or less clearly marked line between what concerns the individual alone and what concerns society as a whole. This is illustrated in the growth from what Spencer called the military type of society to an industrial one. In the case of a militant type of society, to which the religious organization is so closely affiliated, a State is more self contained, and the governing principle is, to use a generalization of Sir Henry Maine's, status rather than contract. With the growth of commerce and industrialism there is developed a greater amount of individual initiative, a growing consideration for personal responsibility, and also the development of a sense of interdependence between societies. And the social developments that go on teach people, even though the lesson may be unconsciously learned, to value each other in terms of social utility rather than in terms of belief in expressed dogmas. They are brought daily into contact with men of widely differing forms of opinion; they find themselves working in the same movements, and participating in the same triumphs or sharing the same defeats. Insensibly the standard of judgment alters; the strength of the purely social feelings overpowers the consciousness of theological differences, and thus serves to weaken the frame of mind from which persecution springs.

The growing complexity of life leads to the same end. Where the conditions of life are simple, and the experiences through which people pass are often repeated, and where, moreover, the amount of positive knowledge current is small, conclusions are reached rapidly, and the feeling of confidence in one's own opinions is not checked by seeing others draw different conclusions from the same premises. Under such conditions an opinion once formed is not easily or quickly changed. Experience which makes for wider knowledge makes also for greater caution in forming opinions and a greater readiness to tolerate conclusions of an opposite character at which others may have arrived.

Finally, on the purely intellectual side one must reckon with the growth of new ideas, and of knowledge that is in itself quite inconsistent with the established creed. If the primary reason for killing the heretic is that he is a social danger, one who will draw down on the tribe the vengeance of the gods, the strength of that feeling against the heretic must be weakened by every change that lessens men's belief in the power of their deity. And one must assume that every time a fresh piece of definite knowledge was acquired towards the splendid structure that now meets us in the shape of modern science there was accomplished something that involved an ultimate weakening of the belief in the supremacy of the gods. The effect is cumulative, and in time it is bound to make itself felt. Religious opinion after religious opinion finds itself attacked and its power weakened. Things that were thought to be solely due to the action of the gods are found to occur without their being invoked, while invocation does not make the slightest difference to the production of given results. Scientific generalizations in astronomy, in physics, in biology, etc., follow one another, each helping to enforce the lesson that it really does not matter what opinions a man may hold about the gods provided his opinions about the world in which he is living and the forces with which he *must* deal are sound and solidly based. In a world where opinion is in a healthy state of flux it is impossible for even religion to remain altogether unchanged. So we have first a change in the rigidity of religious conceptions, then a greater readiness to admit the possibility of error, and, finally, the impossibility of preventing the growth and expression of definitely non-religious and anti-religious opinions in a community where all sorts of opinions cannot but arise.

With the social consequences of religious persecution, and particularly of Christian persecution, I have dealt elsewhere, and there is no need to repeat the story here. I have been here concerned with making plain the fact that persecution does not arise with a misunderstanding of religion, or with a decline of what is vaguely called "true religion," nor does it originate in the alliance of some Church with the secular State. It lies imbedded in the very nature of religion itself. With polytheism there is a certain measure of toleration to gods outside the tribe, because here the admitted existence of a number of gods is part of the order of things. But this tendency to toleration disappears when we come to the monotheistic stage which inevitably treats the claim to existence of other gods in the same spirit as an ardent royalist treats the appearance of a pretender to the throne. To tolerate such is a crime against the legitimate ruler. And when we get the Christian doctrine of eternal damnation and salvation tacked on to the religious idea we have all the material necessary to give the persecutor the feeling of moral obligation, and to make him feel that he is playing the part of a real saviour to society.

At bottom that is one of the chief injuries that a religion such as Christianity inflicts on the race; it throws human feeling into some of the most objectionable forms, and provides a religious and moral justification for their expression. The very desire to benefit one's fellows, normally and naturally healthy, thus becomes under Christian influences an instrument of oppression and racial degradation. The Christian persecutor does not see himself for what he is, he pictures himself as a saviour of men's souls by suppressing the unbeliever who would corrupt them. And if Christianity be true he is correct in thinking himself such. I have no hesitation in saying that if Christianity be true persecution becomes the most important of duties. A community that is thoroughly Christian is bound to persecute, and as a mere matter of historic fact every wholly Christian community has persecuted. The community which says that a man may take any religion he pleases, or go without one altogether if he so chooses, proclaims its disbelief in the importance of religion. The measure of religious freedom is also the measure of religious indifference.

There are some experiences through which a human being may pass the effects of which he never completely outgrows. Usually he may appear to have put them quite out of his mind, but there are times when he is lifted a little out of the normal, and then the recollection of what he has passed through comes back with terrifying force. And acute observers may also be able to perceive that even in normal circumstances what he has passed through manifests itself for the worse in his everyday behaviour. So with religion and the life history of the race. For thousands of generations the race has been under the influence of a teaching that social welfare depended upon a right belief about the gods. The consequence of this has been that persecution became deeply ingrained in human nature and in the social traditions which play so large a part in the character building of each new generation. We have as yet hardly got beyond the tradition that lack of religion robs a man of social rights and dispenses with the necessity for courteous and considered treatment. And there is, therefore, small cause for wonder that the element of intolerance should still manifest itself in connection with non-religious aspects of life. But the certain thing is that throughout the whole of our social history it is religion that has been responsible for the maintenance of persecution as a social duty. Something has been done in more recent times to weaken its force, the growth of science, the rationalizing of one institution after another—in a word, the secularizing of life—is slowly creating more tolerant relations between people. But the poison is deep in the blood, and will not be eradicated in a generation. Religion is still here, and so long as it remains it will never cease—under the guise of an appeal to the higher sentiments of man—to make its most effective appeals to passions of which the best among us are most heartily ashamed.

CHAPTER XVIII
WHAT IS TO FOLLOW RELIGION?

Books on the future of religion are numerous, and to one blessed with a sense of humour, full of entertainment. They are also not without instruction of a psychological kind. Reliable information as to what the future will be like they certainly do not give, but they do unlock the innermost desires of the writers thereof. They express what the writers of the prophecies would like the future to be. And they create the future state on earth exactly as devout believers have built up the character of their heaven beyond the clouds. Every form of faith which they disagree with is rejected as not possessing the element of vitality, with the result that there is only their own form left. And that, they triumphantly proclaim, is the religion of the future.

But the future has an old-fashioned and disconcerting habit of disappointing expectations. The factors that govern human nature are so many and so complex, their transmutations and combinations are so numerous, that it is as well to tread cautiously, and to a very considerable extent leave the future to take care of itself. At the utmost all that we can do with safety is to detect tendencies, and to hasten or retard their development as we think them good or bad. The factors that make up a science of human nature are not to-day so well-known and so well understood that we can depict the state of society a century hence with the same certainty that we can foretell the position of the planet Venus in the year 2000.

My aim in this chapter is, therefore, not to describe precisely what will be the state of society when religious belief has ceased to exist. It is rather to offer a general reply to those gloomy individuals who declare that when the aims of the Freethinker are fully realized we shall find that in destroying religion we have destroyed pretty much all that makes human life worth living. We have managed to empty the baby out with the bath.

The most general form of this fear is expressed in calling Freethought a creed of negation, or a policy of destruction, and assuring the world that mankind can never rest content with such things. That may be quite true, but we fail to see in what way it touches Freethought. A Freethought that is wholly destructive, that is a mere negation, is a creation of the pulpit, and belongs to the same class of imaginative efforts as the pietistic outbursts of famous unbelievers on their death-beds. That such things could have obtained so wide a currency, and be looked upon as quite natural occurrences, offers demonstrative evidence of the paralyzing power of Christian belief on the human mind.

As a matter of fact, neither reformers in general nor Freethinkers in particular deserve the charge of being mere destructionists. They are both far more interested in building up than they are in pulling down, and it is sheer lack of understanding that fixes the eyes of so many on one aspect of the reformer's task and so steadily ignores the other one. Of course, the phenomenon is not an unusual one. In a revolution it is the noise, the street fighting, the breaking of old rules and the shattering of established institutions that attract the most attention. The deeper aims of the revolutionists, the hidden social forces of which the revolution is the expression, the work of reconstruction that is attempted, escape notice. The old order shrieks its loudest at the threat of dissolution, the new can hardly make its voice heard. Carlyle's division of the people into the shrieking thousands and the dumb millions is eternally true. And even the millions are impressed with the importance of the thousands because of the noise they are able to make.

Actually the charge to which reformers in general are open is that of a too great zeal for reconstruction, a belittling of the difficulties that stand in the way of a radical change. They are apt to make too small an allowance for the occurrence of the unexpected and the incalculable, both of which are likely to interfere with the fruition of the most logical of schemes. And they are so obsessed with reconstruction that destruction seems no more than an incident by the way. A little less eagerness for reconstruction might easily result in a greater concern for what is being pulled down. The two greatest "destructive" movements of modern times—the French revolution of 1789 and the Russian revolution—both illustrate this point. In both movements the leading figures were men who were obsessed with the idea of building a new world. They saw this new world so clearly that the old one was almost ignored. And this is equally true of the literature that precedes and is the mouthpiece of such movements. The leading appeal is always to what is to be, what existed is only used as a means of enforcing the desirability of the new order. It is, in short, the mania for reconstruction that is chiefly responsible for the destruction which so horrifies those whose vision can never see anything but the world to which they have become accustomed.

In parenthesis it may be remarked that it is a tactical blunder to make one's attack upon an existing institution or idea depend upon the attractiveness of the ideal state depicted. It enables critics to fix attention on the precise value of the proposed remedy instead of discussing whether the suggested reform is necessary. The attacker is thus placed in the position of the defender and the point at issue obscured. This is, that a certain institution or idea has outgrown its usefulness and its removal is necessary to healthy growth. And it may well be that its removal is all that is required to enable the social organism to function naturally and healthily. The outworn institution is often the grit in the machine that prevents it running smoothly.

This by the way. The fact remains that some of our best teachers have shown themselves apt to stumble in the matter. Without belief in religion they have too often assumed that its removal would leave a serious gap in life, and so would necessitate the creation of a number of substitutes to "take the place of religion." Thus, no less profound a thinker than Herbert Spencer remarks in the preface to his *Data of Ethics*:—

> Few things can happen more disastrous than the death and decay of a regulative system no longer fit, before another and a better regulative system has grown up to replace it. Most of those who reject the current creed appear to assume that the controlling agency furnished by it may safely be thrown aside, and the vacancy left unfilled by any other controlling agency.

Had Spencer first of all set himself to answer the question, "What is it that the Freethinker sets himself to remove?" or even the question, "What is the actual control exerted by religion?" one imagines that the passage above given would either never have been written or would have been differently worded. And when a man such as Spencer permits himself to put the matter in this form one need not be surprised at the ordinary believer assuming that he has put an unanswerable question to the Freethinker when he asks what it is that we propose to put in the place of religion, with the assumption that the question is on all fours with the enquiry as to what substitutes we have for soap and coal if we destroy all stocks of these articles.

The question assumes more than any scientific Freethinker would ever grant. It takes for granted the statement that religion does at present perform some useful function in the State. And that is the very statement that is challenged. Nor does the Freethinker deny that some "controlling agency" is desirable. What he does say is that in the modern State, at least, religion exerts no control for good, that its activities make for stagnation or retrogression, that its removal will make for the healthier operation of other agencies, and that to these other and non-religious agencies belongs the credit which is at present given to religion.

Moreover, Spencer should not have needed reminding that systems of thought while they have any vital relation to life will successfully defy all attempts at eradication. The main cause of the decay of religion is not the attack made upon it by the forces of reasoned unbelief. That attack is largely the conscious expression of a revolt against a system that has long lost all touch with reality, and so has ceased to derive support from current life and thought. From this point of view the reformer is what he is because he is alive to the drift of events, susceptible to those social influences which affect all more or less, and his strength is derived from the thousand and one subtle influences that extend from generation to generation and express themselves in what we are pleased to call the story of civilization.

But the quotation given does represent a fairly common point of view, and it is put in a form that is most favourable to religious pretensions. For it assumes that religion does really in our modern lives perform a function so useful that it would be the height of folly to remove it before we had something equally useful to take its place. But something in the place of religion is a thing that no scientific Freethinker desires. It is not a new religion, or another religion that the world needs, but the removal of religion from the control of life, and a restatement of those social qualities that have hitherto been expressed in a religious form so that their real nature will be apparent to all. Then we shall at last begin to make progress with small chance of getting a serious set-back.

This does not, of course, deny that there are many things associated with religion for the absence of which society would have cause for regret. It is part of the Freethought case that this is so. And it may also be admitted that large numbers of people honestly believe that their religious beliefs serve as motives to the expression of their better qualities. That, again, is part of the delusion we are fighting. We cannot agree that religion, as such, contains anything that is essentially useful to the race. It has maintained its power chiefly because of its association with serviceable social qualities, and it is part of the work of Freethought to distinguish between what properly belongs to religion and what has become associated with it during its long history. At present the confusion exists and the fact need cause no surprise. At best the instincts of man are deep-laid, the motives to conduct are mostly of an obscure kind, and it would be cause for surprise if, seeing how closely religion is associated with every phase of primitive life, and how persistent are primitive modes of thinking, there were not this confusion between the actual part played by religion in life and the part assigned it by tradition.

At any rate, it is idle to argue as though human conduct was governed by a single idea—that of religion. At the most religious beliefs represent no more than a part of the vast mass of influences that determine human effort. And when we see how largely religious beliefs are dependent upon constant stimulation and protection for their existence, it seems extremely unlikely that they can hold a very vital relation to life. The impotency of religion in matters of conduct is, too, decisively shown in the fact that it is quite impossible to arrange men and women in a scale of values that shall correspond with the kind or the fervency of their religious beliefs. A religious person may be a useful member of society or he may be a quite useless one. A profound religious conviction may be accompanied by the loftiest of ideals or by the meanest of aims. The unbeliever may be, and often is, a better man than the believer. No business man would ever think of making a man's religion the condition of taking one into his service, or if he did the general opinion would be that it indicated bigotry and not shrewdness. We find it quite impossible to determine the nature of religious belief by watching the way people behave. In no stage of social life does religion provide us with anything in the nature of a differentiating factor.

It was argued by the late Sir James Fitzjames Stephen, himself a Freethinker, that as men have for a long time been in the habit of associating moral feelings with the belief in God, a severance of the two may entail moral disaster. It is, of course, hard to say what may not happen in certain cases, but it is quite certain that such a consequence could not follow on any general scale. One has only to bring a statement of this kind down from the region of mere theory to that of definite fact to see how idle the fear is. If, instead of asserting in a vague way that the moral life is in some way bound up with religious beliefs we ask what moral action or moral disposition is so connected, we realize the absurdity of the statement. Professor Leuba well says: —

> Our alleged essential dependence upon transcendental beliefs is belied by the most common experiences of daily life. Who does not feel the absurdity of the opinion that the lavish care for a sick child by a mother is given because of a belief in God and immortality? Are love of father and mother on the part of children, affection and serviceableness between brothers and sisters, straightforwardness and truthfulness between business men essentially dependent upon these beliefs? What sort of person would be the father who would announce divine punishment or reward in order to obtain the love and respect of his children? And if there are business men preserved from unrighteousness by the fear of future punishment, they are far more numerous who are deterred by the threat of human law. Most of them would take their chances with heaven a hundred times before they

would once with society, or perchance with the imperative voice of humanity heard in the conscience (*The Belief in God and Immortality*, p. 323).

And in whatever degree the fear may be justified in special cases, it applies to any attempt whatever that may be made to disturb existing conventions. Luther complained that some of his own converts were behaving worse as Protestants than they behaved as Catholics, and even in the New Testament we have the same unfavourable comparison made of many of Christ's followers when compared with the Pagans around them. A transference of allegiance may easily result in certain ill-balanced minds kicking over the traces, but in the long run, and with the mass, the deeper social needs are paramount. There was the same fear expressed concerning man's political and social duties when the relations of Church and State were first challenged. Yet the connection between the two has been quite severed in some countries, and very much weakened in many more, without society in the least suffering from the change. On the contrary, one may say that man's duties towards the State have been more intelligently perceived and more efficiently discharged in proportion as those religious considerations that once ruled have been set on one side.

The reply of the Freethinker to the question of "What is to follow religion?" may, therefore, easily be seen. In effect it is, "Nothing at all." In any study of social evolution the properly equipped student commences his task with the full conviction that whatever the future may be like its germs are already with us. If nature does not "abhor a vacuum" it has at least an intense dislike to absolute beginnings. The future will be an elaboration of the present as the present is an elaboration of the past. For good or evil that principle remains unimpeachable.

The essential question is not, What is to follow religion? but rather what will the disappearance of religion affect that is of real value to the world. The moment the question is raised in this unambiguous manner the answer suggests itself. For assume that by some strange and unexpected happening there set in a raging epidemic of common sense. Assume that as a consequence of this the world was to awake with its mind completely cleared of all belief in religion. What would be the effect of the transformation? It is quite clear that it would not affect any of the fundamental processes of life. The tragi-comedy of life would still be performed, it would run through the same number of acts, and it would end in the same happy or unhappy manner. Human beings would still get born, they would grow up, they would fall in love, they would marry, they would beget their kind, and they would in turn pass away to make room for another generation. Birth and death, with all their accompanying feelings, would remain. Human society would continue, all the glories of art, the greatness of science, all the marvels and wonders of the universe would be there whether we believed in a God or not. The only difference would be that we should no longer associate these things with the existence of a God. And in that respect we should be following the same course of development that has been followed in many other departments of life. We do not nowadays associate the existence of spirits with a good or a bad harvest, the anger of God with an epidemic, or the good-will of deity with a spell of fine weather. Yet in each case there was once the same assumed association between these things, and the same fears of what would happen if that association was discarded. We are only carrying the process a step further; all that is required is a little courage to take the step. In short, there is not a single useful or worthy quality, intellectual or moral, that can possibly suffer from the disappearance of religion.

On this point we may again quote from Professor Leuba:—

> The heroism of religious martyrs is often flaunted as marvellous instances of the unique sustaining strength derived from the belief in a personal God and the anticipation of heaven. And yet for every martyr of this sort there has been one or more heroes who has risked his life for a noble cause, without the comfort which transcendental beliefs may bring. The very present offers almost countless instances of martyrs to the cause of humanity, who are strangers to the idea of God and immortality. How many men and women in the past decade gladly offered and not infrequently lost their lives in the cause of freedom, or justice, or science? In the monstrous war we are now witnessing, is there a less heroic defence of home and nation, and less conscious self-renunciation among the non-believers than among the professed Christians? Have modern nations shown a more intense or a purer patriotism than ancient Greece and Rome, where men did not pretend to derive inspiration for their deeds of devotion in the thoughts of their gods.... The fruitful deeds of heroism are at bottom inspired not by the thought of God or a future life, but by innate tendencies or promptings that have reference to humanity. Self sacrifice, generosity, is rooted in nothing less superficial and accidental than social instincts older than the human race, for they are already present in a rudimentary form in the higher animals.

These are quite familiar statements to all Freethinkers, but to a great many Christians they may come with all the force of a new revelation.

In the earlier pages of this work I have given what I conceive solid reasons for believing that every one of the social and individual virtues is born of human intercourse and can never be seriously deranged for any length of time, so long as human society endures. The scale of values may well undergo a change with the decay of religion, but that is something which is taking place all the time, provided society is not in a state of absolute stagnation. There is not any change that takes place in society that does not affect our view of the relative value of particular qualities. The value we place upon personal loyalty to a king is not what it once was. At one stage a man is ready to place the whole of his fortune at the disposal of a monarch merely because he happens to be his "anointed" king. To-day, the man who had no better reason for doing that would be looked upon as an idiot. Unquestioning obedience to established authority, which once played so high a part in the education of children, is now ranked very low by all who understand what genuine education means. From generation to generation we go on revising our estimate of the value of particular qualities, and the world is the better for the revision. And that is what we may assume will occur with the decay of religious belief. We shall place a higher value upon certain qualities than we do at present and a lower value upon others. But there will be no discarding the old qualities and creation of new ones. Human nature will be the same then as now, as it has been for thousands of years. The nature of human qualities will be more directly conceived and more intelligently applied, and that will be an undesirable development only for those who live by exploiting the ignorance and the folly of mankind.

Thus, if one may venture upon a prophecy with regard to the non-religious society of the future it may be said with confidence that what are known as the ascetic qualities are not likely to increase in value. The cant of Christianity has always placed an excessive value upon what is called self-sacrifice. But there is no value in self-sacrifice, as such. At best it is only of value in exceptional circumstances, as an end it is worse than useless, and it may easily degenerate from a virtue to a vice. It assumed high rank with Christian teachers for various reasons. First, it was an expression of that asceticism which lies at the root of Christianity, second, because Christianity pictured this world as no more than a preparation for another, and taught that the deprivations and sufferings of the present life would be placed to a credit account in the next one, and third, because it helped men and women to tolerate injustice in this world and so helped the political game that governments and the Christian Church have together played. A really enlightened society would rank comparatively low the virtue of asceticism. Its principle would be not self-sacrifice but self-development.

What must result from this is an enlargement of our conception of justice and also of social reform. Both of these things occupy a very low place in the Christian scale of virtues. Social reform it has never bothered seriously about, and in its earlier years simply ignored. A people who were looking for the end of the world, whose teaching was that it was for man's spiritual good to suffer, and who looked for all help to supernatural intervention, could never have had seriously in their minds what we understand by social reform. And so with the conception of Justice. There is much of this in pre-Christian literature, and its entrance into the life and thought of modern Europe can be traced directly back to Greek and Roman sources. But the work of the Christian, while it may have been to heal wounds, was not to prevent their infliction. It was to minister to poverty, not to remove those conditions that made poverty inevitable.

A Spanish writer has put this point so well that I cannot do better than quote him. He says: —

> The notion of justice is as entirely foreign to the spirit of Christianity as is that of intellectual honesty. It lies wholly outside the field of its ethical vision. Christianity — I am not referring to interpretations disclaimed as corruptions or applications which may be set down to frailty and error, but to the most idealized conceptions of its substance and the most exalted manifestations of its spirit — Christianity has offered consolation and comfort to men who suffered under injustice, but of that injustice itself it has remained absolutely incognizant. It has called upon the weary and heavy laden, upon the suffering and the afflicted, it has proclaimed to them the law of love, the duty of mercy and forgiveness, the Fatherhood of God; but in that torment of religious and ethical emotion which has impressed men as the summit of the sublime, and been held to transcend all other ethical ideals, common justice, common honesty have no place. The ideal Christian is seen in the saint who is seen descending like an angel from heaven amid the welter of human misery, among the victims of ruthless oppression and injustice ... but the cause of that misery lies wholly outside the range of his consciousness; no glimmer of right or wrong enters into his view of it. It is the established order of things, the divinely appointed government of the world, the trial laid upon sinners by divine ordinance. St. Vincent

de Paul visits the hell of the French galleys; he proclaims the message of love and calls sinners to repentance; but to the iniquity which creates and maintains that hell he remains absolutely indifferent. He is appointed Grand Almoner to his Most Christian Majesty. The world might groan in misery under the despotism of oppressors, men's lives and men's minds might be enslaved, crushed and blighted; the spirit of Christianity would go forth and *comfort* them, but it would never occur to it to redress a single one of those wrongs. It has remained unconscious of them. To those wrongs, to men's right to be delivered from them, it was by nature completely blind. In respect to justice, to right and wrong, the spirit of Christianity is not so much immoral as amoral. The notion was as alien to it as the notion of truth. Included in its code was, it might be controversially alleged, an old formula, "the golden rule," a commonplace of most literature, which was popular in the East from China to Asia Minor; but that isolated precept was never interpreted in the sense of justice. It meant forgiveness, forbearing, kindness, but never mere justice, common equity; those virtues were far too unemotional in aspect to appeal to the religious enthusiast. The renunciation of life and all its vanities, the casting overboard of all sordid cares for its maintenance, the suppression of desire, prodigal almsgiving, the consecration of a life, the value of which had disappeared in his eyes, to charity and love, non-resistance, passive obedience, the turning of the other cheek to an enemy, the whole riot of these hyperbolic ethical emotions could fire the Christian consciousness, while it remained utterly unmoved by every form of wrong, iniquity and injustice (Dr. Falta de Gracia. Cited by Dr. R. Briffault, *The Making of Humanity*, pp. 334-5.)

That, we may assume, will be one of the most striking consequences of the displacement of Christianity in the social economy. There will be less time wasted on what is called philanthropic work—which is often the most harmful of all social labours—and more attention to the removal of those conditions that have made the display of philanthropy necessary. There will not be less feeling for the distressed or the unfortunate, but it will be emotion under the guidance of the intellect, and the dominant feeling will be that of indignation against the conditions that make human suffering and degradation inevitable, rather than a mere gratification of purely egoistic feeling which leaves the source of the evil untouched.

That will mean a rise in the scale of values of what one may call the intellectual virtues—the duty of truthseeking and truth speaking. Hitherto the type of character held up for admiration by Christianity has been that of the blind believer who allowed nothing to stand in the way of his belief, who required no proofs of its truth and allowed no disproofs to enter his mind. A society in which religion does not hold a controlling place is not likely to place a very high value upon such precepts as "Blessed are those who have not seen and yet have believed," or "Though he slay me yet will I trust him." But a very high value will be placed upon the duty of investigation and the right of criticism. And one cannot easily over-estimate the consequences of a generation or two brought up in an atmosphere where such teachings obtain. It would mean a receptiveness to new ideas, a readiness to overhaul old institutions, a toleration of criticism such as would rapidly transform the whole mental atmosphere and with it enormously accentuate the capacity for, and the rapidity of, social progress.

There is also to be borne in mind the effect of the liberation of the enormous amount of energy at present expended in the service of religion. Stupid religious controversialists often assume that it is part of the Freethinker's case that religion enlists in its service bad men, and much time is spent in proving that religious people are mostly worthy ones. That could hardly be otherwise in a society where the overwhelming majority of men and women profess a religion of some sort. But that is, indeed, not the Freethinker's case at all, and if the badness of some religious people is cited it is only in answer to the foolish argument that religionists are better than others. The real complaint against religion is of a different kind altogether. Just as the worst thing that one can say about a clergyman intellectually is, not that he does not believe in what he preaches, but that he does, so the most serious indictment of current religion is not that it enlists in its service bad characters, but that it dissipates the energy of good men and women in a perfectly useless manner. The dissipation of Christian belief means the liberating of a store of energy for service that is at present being expended on ends that are without the least social value. A world without religion would thus be a world in which the sole ends of endeavour would be those of human betterment or human enlightenment, and probably in the end the two are one. For there is no real betterment without enlightenment, even though there may come for a time enlightenment without betterment. It would leave the world with all the means of intellectual and æsthetic and social enjoyment that exist now, and one may reasonably hope that it will lead to their cultivation and diffusion over the whole of society.

FOOTNOTES:

[1] It will ease my feelings if I am permitted to here make a protest against the shameless way in which this suggestive writer has been pillaged by others without the slightest acknowledgement. They have found him, as Lamb said of some other writers, "damned good to steal from." His series of volumes, *Problems of Life and Mind*, have been borrowed from wholesale without the slightest thanks or recognition.

[2] *Study of Psychology*, pp. 139, 161-5. So again, a more recent writer says: "It is not man himself who thinks but his social community; the source of his thoughts is in the social medium in which he lives, the social atmosphere which he breathes.... The influence of environment upon the human mind has always been recognized by psychologists and philosophers, but it has been considered a secondary factor. On the contrary, the social medium which the child enters at birth, in which he lives, moves and has his being, is fundamental. Toward this environment the individual from childhood to ripest old age is more or less receptive; rarely can the maturest minds so far succeed in emancipating themselves from this medium so far as to undertake independent reflection, while complete emancipation is impossible, for all the organs and modes of thought, all the organs for constructing thoughts have been moulded or at least thoroughly imbued by it" (L. Gumplowicz, *Outlines of Sociology*, p. 157).

[3] *Social Psychology*, pp. 330-1.

[4] "The tyranny exercised unconsciously on men's minds is the only real tyranny, because it cannot be fought against. Tiberius, Ghengis Khan, and Napoleon were assuredly redoubtable tyrants, but from the depths of their graves Moses, Buddha, Jesus, and Mahomet exerted on the human soul a far profounder tyranny. A conspiracy may overthrow a tyrant, but what can it avail against a firmly established belief? In its violent struggle with Roman Catholicism it is the French Revolution that has been vanquished, and this in spite of the fact that the sympathy of the crowd was apparently on its side, and in spite of recourse to destructive measures as pitiless as those of the Inquisition. The only real tyrants that humanity has known have always been the memories of its dead, or the illusions it has forged for itself" (Gustave Le Bon, *The Crowd*, p. 153).

[5] See *Early History of Institutions*, and *Early Law and Custom*.

[6] *Principles of Sociology*, Vol. I.

[7] *Origins of English History*, p. 261.

[8] Speaking of the Inquisition, Mr. H. C. Lea, in his classic *History of the Inquisition*, says, "There is no doubt that the people were as eager as their pastors to send the heretic to the stake. There is no doubt that men of the kindliest tempers, the profoundest aspirations, the purest zeal for righteousness, professing a religion founded on love and charity, were ruthless where heresy was concerned, and were ready to trample it out at any cost. Dominic and Francis, Bonaventure and Thomas Aquinas, Innocent III. and St. Louis, were types, in their several ways, of which humanity, in any age, might feel proud, and yet they were as unsparing of the heretic as Ezzelin di Romano was of his enemies. With such men it was not hope of gain or lust of blood or pride of opinion or wanton exercise of power, but sense of duty, and they but represented what was universal public opinion from the thirteenth to the seventeenth century." Vol. I., p. 234.

[9] This seems to me to give the real significance of Nationality. It has been argued by some that nationality is a pure myth, as unreal as the divinity of a king. The principal ground for this denial of nationality appears to be that so-called national characteristics are seen to undergo drastic transformation when their possessors are subject to a new set of influences. This may be quite true, but if nationality, in the sense of being a product of biological heredity, is ruled out, it does not follow that nationality is thereby destroyed. The fact may remain but it demands a different interpretation. And if what has been said above be true, it follows that nationality is not a personal fact, but an extra or super-personal one. It belongs to the group rather than to the individual, and is created by the possession of a common speech, a common literature, and a common group life. And quite naturally, when the individual is lifted out of this special social influence its power may well be weakened, and in the case of his children may be non-existent, or replaced by the special characteristics of the new group into which he is born. The discussion of nationality ought not, therefore, to move along the lines of acceptance or rejection of the conception of nationality, but of how far specific national characteristics admit of modification under the pressure of new conditions.

[10] It would take too long to elaborate, but it may be here noted that in the human group the impelling force is not so much needs as desires, and that fact raises the whole issue from the level of biology to that of psychology. So long as life is at a certain level man shares with the animal the mere need for food. But at another level there arises not merely the need for food, but a desire for certain kind of food, cooked in a particular manner, and served in a special style. And provided that we do not by hunger reduce man to the level of the beast again, the desire will be paramount and will

determine whether food shall be eaten or not. So, again, with the fact of sex and marriage. At the animal level we have the crude fact of sex, and this is, indeed, inescapable at any stage. But the growth of civilization brings about the fact that the need for the gratification of the sexual appetite is regulated by the secondary qualities of grace of form, or of disposition, which are the immediate determinants of whether a particular man shall marry a particular woman or not. Again, it is the *desire* for power and distinction, not the *need* for money that impels men to spend their lives in building up huge fortunes. And, finally, we have the fact that a great many of our present needs are transformed desires. The working man of to-day counts as needs, as do we all more or less, a number of things that began as pure desires. We say we need books, pictures, music, etc. But none of these things can be really brought under the category of things necessary to life. They are the creation of man's mental cravings. Without them we say life would not be worth living, and it is well that we should all feel so. Professor Marshall rightly dwells upon this point by saying: "Although it is man's wants in the early stages of development that give rise to his activities, yet afterwards each new step is to be regarded as the development of new activities giving rise to new wants, rather than of new wants giving rise to new activities." — (*Principles of Economics*, Vol. I., p. 164.)

[11] It is a curious thing, as Philip Gilbert Hamerton points out in one of his essays, that in England religious freedom appears to exist in inverse proportion to rank. The king has no freedom whatever in a choice of religion. His religion is part of the position. An English nobleman, speaking generally, has two religions from which to choose. He may be either a member of the established Church or of the Roman Catholic. In the middle classes there is the choice of all sorts of religious sects, so long as they are Christian. Religious dissent is permitted so long as it does not travel beyond the limits of the chapel. And when we come to the better class working man, he has the greatest freedom of all. His social position does not depend upon his belonging to this or that Church, and he may, to borrow a phrase from Heine, go to hell in his own fashion.

[12] See specially Vol. I., chapters 6, 7, and 8. One is sorely tempted to engage in what would be a rather lengthy aside on the mental freedom enjoyed by the people of ancient Greece, but considerations of cogency advise a shorter comment in this form. In the first place we have to note that neither the Greeks nor the Romans possessed anything in the shape of "sacred" books. That, as the history of Mohammedanism and Christianity shows, is one of the most disastrous things that can happen to any people. But apart from this there were several circumstances connected with the development of the Greek peoples that made for freedom of opinion. There

was no uniform theology to commence with, and the configuration of the country, while enough to maintain local independence, was not enough to prevent a certain amount of intercourse. And it would certainly seem that no people were ever so devoid of intolerance as were the ancient Greeks. It is true that the history of Greece was not without its examples of intolerance, but these were comparatively few, and, as Professor Bury says, persecution was never organized. The gods were criticized in both speeches and plays. Theories of Materialism and Atheism were openly taught and were made the topic of public discussion. There was, indeed, a passion for the discussion of all sorts of subjects, and to discussion nothing is sacred. The best thought of Rome owed its impetus to Greece, and at a later date it was the recovered thought of Greece which gave the impetus to Mohammedan Spain in its cultivation of science and philosophy, and so led to the partial recovery of Europe from the disastrous control of the Christian Church. Nor need it be assumed that the work of Greece was due to the possession of a superior brain power. Of that there is not the slightest vestige of proof. It is simply that the ancient Greek lived in a freer mental atmosphere. The mind had less to hamper it in its operations; it had no organized and powerful Church that from the cradle to the grave pursued its work of preventing free criticism and the play of enlightened opinion. For several centuries the world has been seeking to recover some of its lost liberties with only a very moderate success. But if one thinks of what the Greeks were, and if one adds to what they had achieved a possible two thousand years of development, he will then have some notion of what the triumph of the Christian Church meant to the world.

[13] See on this point Heeren's *Historical Treatises*, 1836, pp. 61-70.

[14] *Religion and the Child*, Pioneer Press.

[15] Of the evil of an incautious use of current words we have an example in the case of Darwin. Neither his expressions of regret at having "truckled to public opinion" at having used the term "creator," nor his explicit declaration that the word was to him only a synonym of ignorance, prevented religious apologists from citing him as a believer in deity on the strength of his having used the word.

[16] *The Psychological Origin and Nature of Religion*, p. 92.

[17] *Religion as a Credible Doctrine*, p. 11.

[18] *Theism or Atheism*, Chapter 2.

[19] The state of war which normally exists between many, if not most, neighbouring savage tribes, springs in large measure directly from their belief in immortality; since one of the commonest motives to hostility is a desire to appease the angry ghosts of friends who are supposed to have perished by baleful arts of sorcerers in another tribe, and who, if vengeance

is not inflicted on their real or imaginary murderers, will wreak their fury on their undutiful fellow-tribesmen. — *The Belief in Immortality*, Vol. I., p. 468.

[20] It may with equal truth be said that all beliefs are with a similar qualification quite rational. The attempt to divide people into "Rationalists" and "Irrationalists" is quite fallacious and is philosophically absurd. Reason is used in the formation of religious as in the formation of non-religious beliefs. The distinction between the man who is religious and one who is not, or, if it be preferred, one who is superstitious and one who is not, is not that the one reasons and the other does not. Both reason. Indeed, the reasoning of the superstitionist is often of the most elaborate kind. The distinction is that of one having false premises, or drawing unwarrantable conclusions from sound premises. The only ultimate distinctions are those of religionist and non-religionist, supernaturalist and non-supernaturalist, Theist or Atheist. All else are mere matters of compromise, exhibitions of timidity, or illustrations of that confused thinking which itself gives rise to religion in all its forms.

[21] *Aspects of Death in Art and Epigram*, p. 28.

[22] *Golden Bough*, Vol. IV., p. 136.

[23] The question of what are the things that are essential to the welfare of the group, and the fact that individuals are often suppressed for doing what they believe is beneficial to the group, with the kindred fact that there may exist grave differences of opinion on the matter, does not alter the essential point, which is that there must exist sufficient conformity between conduct and group welfare to secure survival.

[24] For this, as well as for the general consequences of persecution on racial welfare, see my pamphlet *Creed and Character*.

[25] I am taking the story of the persecutions of the early Christians for granted, although the whole question is surrounded with the greatest suspicion. As a matter of fact the accounts are grossly exaggerated, and some of the alleged persecutions never occurred. The story of the persecutions is so foreign to the temper of the Roman government as to throw doubt on the whole account. The story of there being ten persecutions is clearly false, the number being avowedly based upon the legend of the ten plagues of Egypt.

[26] The case of Maryland is peculiar. But the reason for the toleration there seems to have been due to the desire to give Catholics a measure of freedom they could not have elsewhere in Protestant countries.

[27] For a good sketch of the Puritan Sunday in New England see *The Sabbath in Puritan New England*, by Alice Morse Earle. For an account of religious intolerance see the account of the Blue Laws of Connecticut as contained in Hart's *American History told by Contemporaries*, Vol. I.